Disciplining Dissent

CAUT SERIES TITLES

Disciplining Dissent, eds. William Bruneau and James L. Turk (2004)

Let Them Eat Prozac by David Healy (2003)

Counting Out the Scholars: How Performance Indicators Undermine Colleges and Universities by William Bruneau and Donald C. Savage (2002)

The Olivieri Report: The Complete Text of the Report of the Independent Inquiry Commissioned by the Canadian Association of University Teachers by Jon Thompson, Patricia Baird, and Jocelyn Downie (2001)

The Corporate Campus: Commercialization and the Dangers to Canada's Colleges and Universities, ed. James L. Turk (2000)

Universities for Sale: Resisting Corporate Control over Canadian Higher Education by Neil Tudiver (1999)

William Bruneau and
James L. Turk, editors

Disciplining Dissent

A CAUT Series Title

James Lorimer & Company Ltd., Publishers

Toronto

© 2004 Canadian Association of University Teachers.

All rights reserved. No part of this book may be reproduced or transmitted in any form or by any means, electronic or mechanical, including photocopying, or by any information storage or retrieval system, without permission in writing from the publisher.

James Lorimer & Company Ltd. acknowledges the support of the Ontario Arts Council. We acknowledge the support of the Government of Canada through the Book Publishing Industry Development Program (BPIDP) for our publishing activities. We acknowledge the support of the Canada Council for the Arts for our publishing program. We acknowledge the support of the Government of Ontario through the Ontario Media Development Corporation's Ontario Book Initiative.

Cover design: Kevin Albert

National Library of Canada Cataloguing in Publication

Disciplining dissent : the curbing of free expression in academia and the media / edited by William Bruneau, James L. Turk.

Co-published by the Canadian Association of University Teachers.
"A CAUT series title".
Includes bibliographical references and index.
ISBN 1-55028-841-5

1. Freedom of speech. 2. Freedom of the press. 3. Academic freedom. 4. Mass media—Censorship. I. Bruneau, William A., 1944– II. Turk, James, 1943–

JC591.D48 2004   323.4'43   C2004-900898-6

A CAUT Series Title
James Lorimer & Company Ltd,
Publishers
35 Britain Street
Toronto, Ontario
M5A 1R7

www.lorimer.ca

Printed and bound in Canada.

Contents

Acknowledgements 6
Preface James L. Turk 7
Introduction *Gillian Steward* 15

Part 1: Keeping Debate Alive 21
1 Publishing the Unpalatable *Patrick O'Neill* 23
2 September 11 and the Failures of American Intellectuals
   Robert Jensen 38

Part 2: Corporate Takeovers: Case Studies 51
3 You Have No Right to Present This Research *David Healy* 53
4 Burying the Messenger *Richard Leitner* 74
5 Industry and Academic Biotechnology: Teaching Students
   the Art of Doublespeak *E. Ann Clark* 105

Part 3: Brave New Workplace 125
6 Beware the Campus CEO *Donald C. Savage* 127
7 The One-Note Chorus *Frances Russell* 134
8 Dissent May Not Need to be Disciplined: Corporate
   Influence in the News Media *Robert A. Hackett* 143

Part 4: Policing Dissent: The New Chill on Campus and in the
   Newsroom 163
9 Students and the Fight for Free Speech in Canada *Ian Boyko* 165
10 Dissent and Collective Action in Oppressive Times
   Aidan White 171

Part 5: Summing Up: Resolve and Respond 183
11 Historical Co-operation between Academics and Journalists
   Jon Thompson 185

About the Authors 191
Notes 196
Bibliography 205
Index 214

Acknowledgements

This book is the sixth in the CAUT Monograph Series. All of the articles took root at meetings sponsored by the Canadian Association of University Teachers (CAUT) and by the Communications, Energy and Paperworkers Union of Canada (CEP). The development of the book and its publication are the result of the commitment and support of the CAUT and the CEP. The editors wish to thank both organizations, especially CAUT's Associate Executive Director, David Robinson, and CEP's National Vice-president for Media, Peter Murdoch. We wish also to thank Jean Lawrence, whose assistance on matters of style and form was indispensable.

Preface
James L. Turk

The fragility of our collective commitment to civil liberties and human rights has once again become worrisomely clear. In the post-9/11 world, governments have introduced draconian anti-terrorism measures that compromise the fundamental liberties that sustain democratic life.

In the United States, the American Civil Liberties Union has sounded a frightening warning:

> There is a pall over our country. In separate but related attempts to squelch dissent, the government has attacked the patriotism of its critics, police have barricaded and jailed protesters, and the New York Stock Exchange has revoked the press credentials of the most widely watched television network in the Arab world. A chilling message has gone out across America: Dissent if you must, but proceed at your own risk.
>
> Government-sanctioned intolerance has even trickled into our private lives. People brandishing anti-war signs or slogans have been turned away from commuter trains in Seattle and suburban shopping malls in upstate New York. Cafeterias are serving

"freedom fries." Country music stations stopped playing Dixie Chicks songs, and the Baseball Hall of Fame cancelled an event featuring "Bull Durham" stars Tim Robbins and Susan Sarandon, after they spoke out against the war on Iraq.[1]

The hastily enacted USA Patriot Act dangerously intermingles law enforcement and intelligence gathering. It impairs public access to vital information. It loosens protections against government invasion of privacy. Federal agents are empowered, for example, to obtain warrants to gather information about the material individuals borrow from libraries or purchase at bookstores—only having to assert that such records may assist in the investigation of terrorism or reveal "other clandestine intelligence"—and anyone served with such a warrant is prohibited from revealing the fact that it has been served.

Government authorities have easier access to confidential student records, and institutions are relieved of the requirement of keeping logs of such requests—logs they must keep for anyone else who asks to see these records. Access to electronic records and files, including email, is substantially eased.

The Bush administration has expanded the number of senior government officials who can designate research as "classified," thereby making it secret. The notion of material that is "sensitive but unclassified" has been resurrected, leading federal agencies to cut off public access to thousands of documents on the Web, to order the withholding of information in government-deposit libraries, and to stop providing information once routinely available to the public.[2]

The new regulations have created serious difficulties for foreign students wishing to study in the United States. Arbitrary detention at borders is common not only for foreign students but also for foreign academics and other travellers, especially those born in countries on the United States' watch list, regardless of their country of citizenship.

Perhaps the best-known story is that of Maher Arar, a Canadian software engineer who was detained by United States authorities when he was in transit at a New York airport en route from a vacation in Tunis to his home in Montreal. Contrary to international law, he was deported by American government officials to Jordan and then sent to Syria, where he was imprisoned and tortured. Only after more than a year in solitary confinement and a massive public campaign was he released and returned to Canada. There a public outcry has forced the Canadian government to launch an inquiry into the complicity of Canadian police and intelligence authorities in his arrest, deportation, and imprisonment in Syria.

The Canadian Association of University Teachers (CAUT) receives several reports a month from members who have been arbitrarily detained at American border crossings, especially academics who are Canadian citizens but were born in Islamic countries.

Like the United States, in December 2001 Canada quickly passed its Anti-Terrorism Act without much debate. Canada's legislation grants police expanded investigative and surveillance authority. It allows for preventive detention and investigative hearings. It undermines the principle of due process by keeping certain information of "national interest" from being disclosed during judicial proceedings. It allows individuals and organizations *suspected* of terrorist links ("terrorist" being vaguely and expansively defined) to be placed on a list and subjected to severe measures. The legislation also provides for the issuance of security certificates and secret trials.

In anticipation of the legislatively mandated three-year review of the Anti-Terrorism Act, Roch Tassé, coordinator of Canada's International Civil Liberties Monitoring Group, has observed that the Act "appears to have proven not that useful, nor necessary, in the fight against international terrorists, but has served instead to intimidate domestic political dissent and members of racial and religious minorities."[3]

As in the United States, Canada's Anti-Terrorism Act is just one of many legislative, regulatory, and procedural initiatives that has the effect of trampling on taken-for-granted Canadian civil liberties and privacy rights. The Canadian government has agreed to work with the United States to compile a database of all air travellers, whether on domestic or transborder flights, and to establish an "air-scoring" system for assigning "risk" ratings to travellers, resulting in those rated "red" being banned from air travel.

The larger American goal is to collect and retain personal information on all citizens on the planet. This massive database will allow total surveillance of all travellers. Tassé notes that over the past two years, the American government has acquired access to data on hundreds of millions of residents of ten Latin American countries through a private company called Choice Point. The information acquired includes the entire voter registry of Mexico as well as Colombia's entire citizen-ID database. Choice Point's subsidiary, Database Technologies, is the company responsible for the reorganization of the electoral list in Florida that led to George W. Bush's victory in 2000.

In other measures, the Canadian government has announced it plans to ease restrictions on the interception of electronic communication by police, regulators, and security intelligence officials. Government plans call for production, assistance, and data preservation orders that will require all Internet service providers to locate, collect, and deliver to state authorities any information stored in their systems; to assist state authorities in any way necessary to carry out authorized interception or search and seizure; and to store and save existing data that are specific to a transaction or client for as long as it takes state authorities to obtain a "production" order or a warrant to seize the data.

Canadian officials have made clear they want Canada to meet the US demand for travel documents with biometric identifiers and, going further, to introduce a mandatory ID card, with biometric identifiers, that every resident would have to carry at all times. Such a card would give authorities access to a wide range of personal information; the scheme raises serious questions about Canadians' privacy rights. In its brief to the House of Commons, the Canadian Bar Association cautioned:

> Although there have been suggestions that a National Identity Card will address identity theft and enhance security, no analysis has been provided about the specific impact that a National Identity Card can be expected to have on either of these problems, nor why a national identity card is the preferred solution over other potential solutions. This is particularly troubling given the far-reaching impact of a National Identity Card on the privacy of Canadians.[4]

Preface

Whether it be biometric identifiers, national ID cards, wider powers of surveillance for police and intelligence agencies, sharing personal data, or lower thresholds for access to electronic records, Canada is taking its lead from the United States. Such initiatives feed a mood of insecurity and encourage the abandonment of long-cherished civil liberties.

In a chilling example of the way civil liberties and basic human rights can be redefined as "the problem," the Federal Research Division of the Library of Congress issued a report on *Nations Hospitable to Organized Crime and Terrorism*. In its section on Canada, the report says:

> As a modern liberal democracy Canada possesses a number of features that make it hospitable to terrorists and international criminals. The Canadian Constitution guarantees rights such as the right to life, liberty, freedom of movement, freedom of speech, protection against unreasonable search and seizure, and protection against arbitrary detention or imprisonment that make it easier for terrorists and international criminals to operate.[5]

After reviewing Canada's anti-terrorist initiatives since 9/11, the report notes ominously:

> Whether these new laws are effective in reducing the use of Canada as an operational base and transit country for terrorists and international criminals will depend in large part on whether a new balance between civil liberties and security concerns will yield effective prevention.[6]

Not since the cold war years of the 1940s and 1950s have there been such menacing threats to the civil libertarian underpinnings of democratic society. These threats create special concerns in the two institutions that are democracies' guardians of free expression and critical thought and inquiry—universities and the media.

Universities' lifeblood is academic freedom—the freedom of inquiry and research, freedom of teaching, freedom of expression and dissent, freedom to publish, freedom to express opinions about the institution in which one works. All these freedoms are to be exercised without reference to orthodoxy, conventional wisdom, or fear of repression from the state or any other source. Without these freedoms, universities cannot fulfill their function of discovering knowledge, disseminating that knowledge to their students and the society at large, and instilling in their students a mature independence of mind.

Likewise, democracy depends on a free, independent, and critical media. In his book *Democracy's Oxygen,* James Winter likens the human need of oxygen for survival to the need of democracy for free media. Democracy will die without the oxygen of free media.[7]

In the face of anti-terrorism initiatives that are shrinking the space for critical thought and dissent, universities and the media have to assert their right to freedom of thought and expression more aggressively than ever. Regrettably, their ability to fulfill their historic role is being circumscribed at this critical juncture by growing corporate control of both universities and the media. Concentration in media ownership is staggering. Less than a dozen giant transnational corporations control the majority of the world's newspapers, radio and television broadcasters, movies, and magazines. Voices are stifled as giant corporations take over independent media.

In whole regions of Canada and the United States, there are no competing newspapers. Looser restrictions on cross-media ownership have helped ensure the disappearance of diverse opinions. For journalists, this consolidation has often meant suppression of their freedom of expression, as there are few alternative employers to turn to should they dissent *too* effectively from the corporate view of the owner or the corporate advertisers that provide so much revenue. With reduced staffing levels, journalists find they rarely have the time and resources to engage in investigative reporting and dig out stories that go beyond scandal or perspectives fed them by governments, corporations, and powerful organizational interests.

In universities, corporate-dominated boards choose presidents who try to impose command-and-control management styles on university governance, thus marginalizing academic staff. Cutbacks in government funding have made university administrators particularly receptive to corporate donors and sponsors who often want a greater say in university priorities. Necessary research is increasingly dependent on corporate funding, often with priority to the corporation's financial benefit. As we have seen in the case of Nancy Olivieri[8] and many others, the consequence has been attempts (all too often successful) to suppress "unfavourable" research despite the harmful repercussions of any such suppression for the public interest. Researchers who swim against the corporate tide often find their academic careers threatened.[9]

Disciplining Dissent considers these important questions from the inside. Leading academics and journalists examine the pressures that limit freedom of expression and make it increasingly difficult for universities and the media to fulfill their duty to keep critical thought and free expression alive. The issues raised in this book are especially compelling at the present historical moment, when civil liberties and human rights are endangered in ways we have not seen for fifty years.

Introduction
Gillian Steward

When I first thought about the theme of this volume, I wondered if journalists and academics would be able to tackle it without an ugly eruption of underlying tension. Academics often view journalists as superficial gadflies, while journalists see academics as woolly thinkers who take forever to get to the point.

But instead of emphasizing their differences, the two groups have found common cause and common ground—an indication, no doubt, of the plight in which both academics and journalists find themselves these days. Journalists are hampered by media owners seeking efficiency and profit. Academics are hampered by university administrators who see commercialization of research as one of the best ways to increase revenue.

Without free expression for journalists, academics have less opportunity to bring their ideas and research to the public's attention. If academics are constrained, journalists are denied the material they need for investigative or analytical stories. Hence the common cause is based on the reality of the work we do. Without freedom of expression it is all but impossible for either academics or journalists to accomplish much. This deep frustration fuelled an intense and lively discussion on the state of free expression in Canada.

As I read the papers in *Disciplining Dissent*, I can't help but think how many other people will wish to see them. Who wouldn't be interested in Ann Clark's revelations on the doublespeak used in the genetically modified seeds debate? Or the behind-the-scenes manipulation by the pharmaceutical industry that David Healy writes of? Who wouldn't want to know about all the power games associated with a simple garbage dump that journalist Richard Leitner has illuminated?

So much of this goes to the heart of a malaise that affects more than just academics and journalists. Canadians may be less deferential than they were a decade or so ago, but they are also more alienated from the levers of power. Frances Russell, a columnist for the *Winnipeg Free Press*, suggests there is a huge gap between what most Canadians want of their governments and what they actually get. In poll after poll, survey after survey, said Russell, Canadians cite public health care and education as high priorities and yet the governments they elect prioritize balanced budgets, debt repayment, and tax cuts. The agenda of big business always prevails no matter the political party elected to govern. Big media has adopted the same agenda and shamelessly promotes it rather than questioning the gulf between the street and the elite, said Russell. Media owners always used editorials to promote their pro-business views, but now they expect newsroom journalists to toe the line as well. Consequently, the views of the elite dominate all mainstream media, all the time, and are always presented as inevitable.

All of this is familiar to the writers from academia represented here. Donald Savage writes of "Campus CEOs" rolling back the freedoms gained in the 1960s and replacing them with autocratic governance "dressed up in fancy new managerial language." He points to trends in New Zealand in the 1980s exported to North America by those anxious to turn universities into research and training facilities designed to serve the interests of big business. Robert Jensen from the University of Texas laments the apathy of US academics during the post-9/11 era: "The fundamental failure of US universities after 9/11 was the unwillingness to take seriously their role as centers of knowledge and their refusal to create space for discussion." Jensen blamed the apathy on the "market model" university, a place where research grants and status are more important than ideas and debate.

Patrick O'Neill thinks things aren't much better in Canada. He cites three examples of controversial articles published in academic journals that elicited calls for censorship from other academics and politicians. "In all three cases, a substantial group of critics argued the authors' views were not only in error but should never have been published," says O'Neill. But at least professors have tenure—they can't be fired for saying unpopular things. Students are much more vulnerable. And according to Ian Boyko of the Canadian Federation of Students, the clampdown on student resistance was well underway long before 9/11. At the 1997 Asia-Pacific Economic Cooperation (APEC) conference in Vancouver and the Organization of American States (OAS) conference in Windsor in June 2001, students were subject to pre-emptive arrest, campuses were flooded with police officers in riot gear. The campus is no longer a "free space," writes Boyko.

Some writers define the central problem as a battle between left and right. Although this is a valid perspective, I am not inclined to cast it that way. Perhaps that's because I'm from Alberta, the one-party state. Nevertheless, I believe that if we go down this road we will get stuck. For as I read Ann Clark, David Healy, Richard Leitner, and others, I can't help but think we are talking about something much more fundamental than a battle between the left and the right—something all kinds of people can agree on, or find common cause with.

We are talking about Honesty. Integrity. Equity. Justice. Independence. Trust. Courage. On the negative side of the ledger we are talking about Dishonesty. Lying. Corruption. Abuse of power. Manipulation. Censorship. Greed.

In the present era these words have become somewhat "corny" or "quaint." Just saying them may invite disdain, another sign of the stunning descent of ethical values we have witnessed over the past decade or so. Before the descent, individuals, corporations, and governments were much more careful about hiding their ethical transgressions because they did not represent an acceptable way of doing things. But now we see companies like Enron (Johnson, 2004) and WorldCom (Stern, 2004) and our own governments and politicians engage in blatantly unethical—sometimes criminal—activities with a kind of pride. It's as though conflict of interest is now seen as a way of getting ahead, of making even more money. And to many that's a good thing, not a bad thing. Conflict of interest has now been built into the system to such an extent that for many people it is simply hard to avoid. So rather than fight it, they decide to profit from it.

But in this self-serving environment we would be wise to heed the question that David Healy asks: "Who are you?" When the doctor takes off his white coat, who is he? When the journalists puts down her notebook, who is she? When the professor and the student leave the classroom, who are they? What do they value?

If we approach these problems in terms of values, I think we have an opportunity to expand the tent, to include a lot of other people in this discussion. Just as Aidan White says, we must connect with people and organizations that have shared values and agendas. And as Bob Hackett says, we need to collaborate with people who are also concerned about these issues because there is strength in numbers. Looking at these problems as an attack on the values we hold to be important gives us an opportunity to do that. We also need to devise practical ways to advance those values and agendas. White points out that codes of conduct, declarations, and manifestos amount to nothing if there are no practical ways to implement them. Academics need to organize in the same way the International Federation of Journalists has organized: they can now respond quickly whenever a journalist anywhere in the world is imprisoned or censured in some way. This is an immensely effective means of supporting each other while at the same time pointing out infringements on freedom of expression or freedom of the press. We can offer support in small ways too. If someone takes a risk or makes a brave public stand, phone them up and thank them. This kind of support can make a huge difference.

There are also structural changes on which we should insist. We can push for stronger public broadcasting and strong legislation to control cross-ownership of media. Perhaps we should have tax incentives for start-up publications that want to deal in a diversity of views on issues of public interest. We should press for many of the measures proposed by writers in this book: more independent research; legislation to protect whistle-blowers; legislation to ensure better access to information;

more government capacity for research. We could work to weaken the connection of money to power in politics, as Frances Russell suggests. We certainly ought to promote the idea of government as countervail to other powerful forces, as Ann Clark proposes.

It is easy to sink into despair in the face of the obstacles and work required to achieve what we want. But despair is not an option. Instead we must use the power we have, power that so many others do not have. For example, I would urge professors who have tenure to use that gift to speak out on controversial issues. There are not many people in Canada who can say whatever they want with no fear of losing their jobs.

I would also urge journalists to speak to people in the communities they serve about the problems they are facing in the newsroom. Journalists traditionally distance themselves from people in the community in order to be objective, so they can't be accused of showing fear or favour to any one group. And it is still necessary for them to do that. But I think journalists need to speak to their friends and neighbours about what is going on in newsrooms. I'm not suggesting whine-fests but rather a simple explanation of how current media practices affect them. If certain stories are being suppressed either through lack of resources or outright censorship, people need to know about it. Decisions about what is and what is not in the news affects them in a very direct way. Journalists need to forge some bonds in the community that go beyond the bonds needed for news gathering.

The papers published here were first offered publicly some six months before the United States' invasion of Iraq. But war was in the air and it lent a certain urgency, and gloominess, to the proceedings. Talk of censorship and apathy on campuses in the United States added to the sense that this war was inevitable, whether it was justified or not. And if the United States went to war, surely Canada would too. In the ensuing months Canadian elites, including most of the mainstream media, pushed for Canada to join the invasion. Week after week Canadians were subjected to news stories about preparations for war, about the imminent threat from weapons of mass destruction. Nevertheless, the majority of Canadians steadfastly opposed participation by Canada without the sanction of the United Nations. Their

Prime Minister agreed with them and kept Canada out of the fray. I, for one, felt encouraged. It seemed that dissent was alive and well in Canada despite all official attempts to discipline it.

It's important to remember that we will always have to struggle for freedom of expression and other rights attached to liberal democracy. It's not as though we can win this battle and then sit back and relax. There will always be forces at play who do not see democratic society as an advantage to their particular interests. But even though the struggle is a never-ending one and often difficult, it is fundamental to our well-being. And if at times we need to be buoyed we must remember that without this struggle, our lives, and the lives of others, would be greatly diminished.

Part I
Keeping Debate Alive

1
Publishing the Unpalatable
Patrick O'Neill

Voltaire is credited with this aphorism: "I disagree with every word you say but will defend to the death your right to say it." Although the quote is not quite accurate, it has served to express the credo of those who champion freedom of speech, however unpopular the content.

According to that credo, we are supposed to tolerate expression of a wide variety of opinions, even if we find some of those opinions outrageous, perhaps disgusting—dangerous. Rather than suppress, we are invited to reply.

Recently, some of those outrageous opinions have been set forth as conclusions derived from empirical research. They have called forth not only methodological critiques but also demands for censorship and suppression. Sometimes, it seems, our determination to "defend to the death" someone's right to say something is sorely tested. In the following three cases, controversial findings, conclusions, or opinions by researchers tested the credo.

A Racial Hierarchy
In 1989, J. Philippe Rushton, a psychology professor at the University of Western Ontario, gave a speech to the annual meeting of the

American Association for the Advancement of Science (AAAS) entitled "Evolutionary Biology and Heritable Traits." He referred to three broad groupings of human population (in his terms, Mongoloids, Caucasoids, Negroids) as having emerged at different times from the ancestral hominid line. Natural selection, he suggested, had favoured the more recently evolved Mongoloids; disadvantaged the Negroids, who were most genetically distant; and left Caucasoids in between the other two.

Based on this theory, Professor Rushton presented a cornucopia of genetically based racial differences that favoured Asians, disparaged Blacks, and made Whites intermediate. These differences were said to include brain size and intelligence, millions of excess neurons, maturational delay, sexual restraint, and social organization. Critics were quick to call this theory racist considering Professor Rushton was producing data from various sources that purported to show Blacks had smaller brains and were less intelligent; had intercourse more frequently and were more likely to spread sexually transmitted diseases such as AIDS; had unstable marriages and were more likely to break the law; and were more aggressive, less sociable, and more prone to mental illness. Furthermore, these differences—if they were shown to exist—were supposed to be genetic rather than environmental.

After his controversial speech to the AAAS, Professor Rushton continued to expound his thesis in various journals (for instance, Rushton, 1991) and drew fire from those who criticized both his methods and his conclusions. Some questioned his application of evolutionary theory to human racial groups (for instance, Anderson, 1991). Others identified flaws in sources he used in his meta-analyses (for instance, Weizmann, Wiener, Wiesenthal, & Ziegler, 1990; 1991). He and his critics went back and forth over the question of whether some of his source material constituted "ethnopornography" (for instance, Rushton, 1991; Weizmann et al., 1991).

In any event, Professor Rushton admitted that the original studies contained "numerous sources of error," but he was not particularly concerned. He argued that his analysis relied on his "principle of aggregation" (1991, p. 31), according to which the sum of a set of multiple measurements is a more stable and unbiased estimator than any single measurement from the set. If you have enough studies from enough sources, the flaws in individual studies cancel each other out.

Another source of controversy was Professor Rushton's reliance on the concept of race, which he used in a way that many found outmoded. Critic Frederic Weizmann and his colleagues (1990) complained that the tripartite race classification had been widely discredited as a biological concept. Professor Rushton replied that his classification of countries on the basis of race showed general patterns to emerge, and that those patterns, in turn, validated the classification system.

Such exchanges between Professor Rushton and his critics were typical of the sort of debate that is supposed to ensure that science is self-correcting. But some commentators took the argument to a different level: they called for censorship and suppression—demanding that his papers not be published, that he be denied research funding from public sources, and that he no longer be permitted to teach.

Biologist David Suzuki said, "By defending Dr. Rushton's right to pronounce and spread his ideas, the academic community is besmirched by shoddy science and stands condemned for a dereliction of its social responsibility" (1989, p. D4).

The University of Western Ontario kept Professor Rushton physically out of the classroom for a time, showing his lectures to students on videotape. Some thought this measure did not go far enough. Ontario's premier of the day, David Peterson, joined the chorus of those wanting Western to fire the professor (Horn, 1999).

Nineteen individuals, mainly students, filed a complaint with the Ontario Human Rights Commission. They alleged that Professor Rushton had "poisoned the academic learning environment" at Western. They demanded that he be fired; that any teaching of theories about racial hierarchies be prohibited; that the university be required to examine its entire curriculum and eliminate so-called "academic racism" to ensure that the curriculum reflected the province's ethnic diversity; and that "racist research" be prohibited at the university.

The Academic Freedom and Tenure Committee of the Canadian Association of University Teachers (CAUT), of which I was then a member, voted to seek intervener status if and when the human rights case was heard. The committee was concerned about the breadth of the complaint and the chill that the case might impose on free inquiry and scholarship on controversial topics.

The opportunity to intervene never came. The Human Rights Commission was finally ready to proceed in late 1995, more than four years after the complaint had been filed. It attempted to notify the parties, but letters addressed to eleven of the nineteen complainants were returned, marked "address unknown." All the returned letters belonged to students. The Human Rights Commission considered the case abandoned.

Women Who Work
In 1990, chemistry professor Gordon Freeman from the University of Alberta published a paper in the *Canadian Journal of Physics* entitled "Kinetics of nonhomogeneous processes in human society: Unethical behaviour and social chaos" (Freeman, 1990). Professor Freeman was concerned about the apparent increase in cheating in his large first-year courses. He talked to his students in groups as large as 250, and on the basis of these discussions he concluded:

- the tendency to cheat is correlated strongly with the absence of a full-time mother in the home when the child was growing up;

- mothers entering the work force show a lack of maternal loyalty to their children, who are "treated as objects both by parents and by caregivers"; and

- children of working mothers are at increased risk "for drug abuse, compulsive eating, not telling the truth, and other socially destabilizing behaviour" (pp. 796–797).

The article appeared in a special issue devoted to a conference on chaos theory; it appeared under the label "Sociology." Those attending the chaos theory conference, however, could not remember the paper being presented.

As in the Rushton case, there were debates about the validity of the findings. Sociologist Marlene Mackie said that Professor Freeman's paper ignored decades of social science research, substituted informal chats for rigorous methods, and violated "the scientific canons of empiricism, skepticism, objectivity, and logical reasoning" (quoted in Montagnes, 1993, p. 197).

In his original article, the chemistry professor seemed to present himself as a champion of qualitative methods: "Information gained by surveys and experiments with controls is likely to be distorted by the artificiality of the gathering situation" (Freeman, 1990, p. 796). To have conclusions such as Professor Freeman's cloaked in the mantle of qualitative research was almost more than some qualitative researchers could bear. Cannie Stark, speaking for the Canadian Psychological Association, said, "Qualitative research, responsibly conducted, is scientific and can be a very rewarding source of rich, meaningful data on important issues." But, she said, Professor Freeman had confounded hypothesis generation with hypothesis testing and had attributed causation to potentially spurious correlations: "As they stand, no credence should be given to Freeman's conclusions" (quoted in Montagnes, 1993, p. 197).

Again, over and above this sort of debate, there were complaints that the original article was published in the first place. It was, after all, an article by a chemist, published in a journal of physics, purporting to be sociology, treating a topic that was arguably psychological. The journal editor said he published the piece because he mistakenly believed it had been presented at a conference. But he also took a more politically engaged stand; he was quoted in *Science* as blaming "political correctness" and "vulgar politics of protest" for the strong reaction against publication of the article (Montagnes, 1993, p. 200).

In June 1991, the *Canadian Journal of Physics* published an apology over the signature of Bruce P. Dancik, editor-in-chief of all National Research Council (NCR) journals. Professor Dancik said that Professor Freeman's article did not comprise science and had no place in a scientific journal. "The National Research Council Research Journals and the Editor of the *Canadian Journal of Physics* regret that this article was published" (Dancik, 1991, p. 1403).

But was it enough to regret publication? Could the article be "unpublished"? Some critics wanted all copies of the journal recalled and reissued

Disciplining Dissent

absent of any trace of the brief foray into "sociology." One such group was the Women in Physics Committee of the Canadian Association of Physicists, who called on the NRC to require the journal to withdraw the offending issue "in order to have it replaced with a corrected copy" (quoted in Sheinen, 1993, p. 245). The notion of expunging the written record was rejected by Editor-in-Chief Dancik, who said, "in addition to being impractical, [this] would be sweeping the article under the carpet and would be an attempt to rewrite history" (Dancik, 1993, p. 271).

In the face of growing pressure to do something, the NRC offered to print a special supplement of the journal with commentaries on the controversy from social scientists. But then, with some invited contributions already in hand, the NRC changed its mind. The editor-in-chief said that if the physics journal was not an appropriate place to publish the original article, then it was also not the appropriate place to debate it (Dancik, quoted in Dahlin, 1993, p. 9). Stephen Prudhomme, director of research journals at the NRC, said the council wanted to give the Freeman article as little media exposure as possible (quoted in Wolfe, 1991, D1). Clive Willis, the NRC's Vice-President (Science), said that publication of the supplement would "give Freeman a day in court, and that is the last thing we want" (quoted in Dahlin, 1993, p. 9).

The decision not to publish drew responses ranging from surprise to outrage. In response, the NRC changed its mind yet again and re-scheduled publication of the supplement. Between these two decisions, the embattled NRC held a two-day conference on "The Ethics of Scholarly Publishing." At that meeting, the agency was roundly criticized for its handling of the Freeman affair and for the loose policies that governed the journals it published.

The week after the symposium, the NRC approved a new policy governing authors, editors, and referees. Among other things, the policy directed that "It is the responsibility of authors to ensure that the language used is inclusive and that gender and racial stereotyping are avoided" (National Research Council of Canada, 1993, p. 275).

As in the Rushton case, students became involved. *Gateway*, the student newspaper at the University of Alberta, reported that students were taking up a petition demanding that Professor Freeman either apologize or resign his academic post (Sheinin, 1993).

Sex with Children

In 1998, Rind, Tromovitch, and Bauserman published an article in the prestigious *Psychological Bulletin* entitled "A meta-analytic examination of assumed properties of child sexual abuse using college samples." The authors analyzed studies with a combined sample size of 50,000.

They reported that the relationship between being a victim of child abuse and later psychopathology was weak or negligible. The correlations were particularly low when the sexual relationship was between males and was deemed "consensual" by the minors. The authors even reported that some children experienced positive results in "willing" sexual encounters with adults (Rind, Tromovitch, & Bauserman, 1998).

As in the previous two cases, there was lively debate with regard to method and conclusions. Critics argued that college samples probably exclude those with severe pathology, biasing the outcome toward finding no effect of early trauma (Dallum et al., 2001). The authors replied that their college-student samples were more representative of the general population than the clinical and forensic samples used in research that had shown pathological outcomes (Rind, Tromovitch, & Bauserman, 2001).

Some critics said that because children cannot legally consent to sexual activity with adults, the "consent" variable was scientifically meaningless and ethically dubious. The authors replied that the legal status of "consent" and the perception by minors that they were willing participants are two different issues. They noted that whether an event causes psychological damage is a separate question from whether it is "wrong" (Rind et al., 2001).

The article was subjected to spin from opposing camps. It was hailed by advocates of "man-boy love," condemned by a group advocating aggressive corrective treatment for homosexuality, and attacked most famously by Dr. Laura Schlessinger, a physiologist with a popular radio talk show. Dr. Laura said, "the point of the article is to allow men to rape male children" (quoted in Lilienfeld, 2002). Her vigorous campaign against the American Psychological Association (APA) as publisher of *Psychological Bulletin* reached an estimated 18 million listeners—and the ears of the United States Congress. A precedent-setting resolution condemning the article, the journal, and the APA was introduced in the

House of Representatives—the only known instance in which a specific scientific article has been singled out for censure in a congressional resolution, or a scientific organization chastised for publishing such an article.

Representative Matt Salmon (Arizona), introducing House Concurrent Resolution 107, condemned the Rind et al. article as "the emancipation proclamation of pedophiles." According to Resolution 107, "The *Psychological Bulletin* has recently published a severely flawed study.... Congress condemns and denounces all suggestion in the article that indicate that sexual relationships between adults and 'willing' children are less harmful than believed, and condemns any suggestion that sexual relations between children and adults ... are anything but harmful" (Lilienfeld, 2002, p. 181).

During congressional consideration, the APA desperately passed internal resolutions condemning child sexual abuse and appealed to sister organizations for help. The organization asked the National Academy of Sciences (NAS) and the American Association for the Advancement of Science (AAAS) to indicate publicly that APA journals are respected in the scientific community, that their peer review is rigorous, and that the scientific process is self-correcting. Both organizations refused to get involved.

In fact, some scientific organizations took pains to dissociate themselves from APA. The American Psychiatric Association pointed out that they were a different group from the psychologists (both groups are called "APA"). They indicated that one difference between the organizations was that the *psychiatrists* were opposed to pedophilia. This unhelpful clarification was sent, with the psychiatrists' apparent approval, to all members of the House of Representatives (Garrison & Kobor, 2002).

When the APA tried to mollify Congress it created an uproar among its own members. Raymond Fowler, chief executive officer of the APA, sent a letter to influential congressman Representative Tom DeLay. Fowler said that the Rind et al. piece "included opinions of the authors that are inconsistent with APA's stated and deeply held positions ... sexual activity between children and adults should never be considered or labelled harmless" (Fowler, 1999, p. 1). The letter said that the Rind et al. article should have been evaluated for its potential for misinforming the public policy process: "This is something we failed to do, but will do in the future" (p. 1). It promised that APA would strengthen procedures to address the social policy implications of journal articles. The editor and action editor who handled the Rind et al. article for *Psychological Bulletin* refer to this as the "capitulation letter" (Sher & Eisenberg, 2002, p. 209). Angry APA members protested that the organization was proposing to censure articles and to interfere with the peer review process.

As Congress prepared to vote on Resolution 107, the APA went back to the AAAS for support—one of the influential scientific organizations that had earlier spurned the plea for support. Now, the APA asked the AAAS to review and evaluate the scientific quality of the article. Again, many APA members were outraged, seeing the request as undermining the APA's own journal review process. The AAAS eventually declined, commenting that there was "no reason to second guess the process of peer review used by the APA journal in its decision to publish" (quoted in Sher & Eisenberg, 2002, p. 207).

The congressional resolution passed 355 to 0 in the House and by a voice vote in the Senate. No member of Congress voted against the resolution.

Even after the public controversy had subsided, the waters continued to roil within the psychological community. Scott Lilienfeld of Emory University submitted an article on the controversy to the *American Psychologist*, the flagship journal of the APA. His piece was called "The bonfires of the vilifiers: Dr. Laura, the US Congress, the American Psychological Association, and the Rind et al. (1998) Sexual Abuse Meta-Analysis."

Professor Lilienfeld analyzed the original article, methodological criticisms of it, the public furor, and what he considered to be the APA's backing away from defending its editorial process, including its decision to ask the AAAS for a belated external review. Lilienfeld's article was evaluated by four reviewers. Following some requested revisions, in February 2001 the action editor accepted the article for publication. The overall editor, Richard McCarty, was copied on the e-mail and congratulated Professor Lilienfeld. But he then overruled the decision to accept. Without informing either the author or the action editor, he sent the article for "re-review" by five more reviewers. He has said that he knew in advance that at least three of the five would "have concerns with the manuscript" (McCarty, 2002, p. 199).

On the basis of all nine reviews, he informed the author that the original acceptance had been overturned and the article had been re-reviewed. He also asked for "changes of a substantive nature." According to Professor Lilienfeld, the changes would have deleted 60 percent of the article, including all material dealing with the Rind et al. controversy, all material critical of the APA and the actions of the APA during the incident, and all material critical of the actions of members of Congress. The author considered the requested changes tantamount to a rejection of his previously accepted article.

The wounded author took his story to the Web. Many prominent psychologists threatened to resign in protest against the perceived "politicizing" of the editorial process. What now became known as the "Lilienfeld controversy" threatened to do as much damage within the APA as the Rind et al. controversy had done to the organization from the outside. Summing up the impact of both controversies, Kenneth J. Sher and Nancy Eisenberg, the *Psychological Bulletin* editors who handled the original article, called the whole matter "the greatest public relations disaster and threat to its well-being that the APA has ever faced" (Sher & Eisenberg, 2002, p. 209).

Arguments Usual and Unusual
In the three cases above, controversial material was presented in the form of research findings. Highly respected organizations: the American Association for the Advancement of Science, the National Research Council of Canada, and the American Psychological Association were involved as publishers or conference sponsors. In each case there was debate about method and conclusions of the sort one might expect in the self-correcting nature of scientific inquiry.

Less usual was the focus of some critics on the authors' motivation. In all three cases, the authors were alleged to have biases that compromised their objectivity. Professor Rushton received substantial funding from the Pioneer Fund, an American group dedicated to advancing eugenics.

Professor Freeman was said to be driven by an anti-feminist agenda. Among the social evils he thought resulted from women at work he included feminism, which he associated with socialism. Although Professor Freeman said he was "non-judgmental" (p. 795), this posture was somewhat undercut by his circulation, at the height of the controversy, of an unpublished paper arguing against more women in science (Montagnes, 1993).

Rind et al. were accused of displaying their true colours when they suggested that the term "child sexual abuse" might better be replaced by "adult-child sex." One of the authors was also attacked for having published in a Dutch journal that had featured articles tolerant of pedophilia (Garrison & Kobor, 2002).

In all three cases a substantial group of critics argued that the views expressed by the authors were not only in error but should never have been expressed at all. And, if the authors chose to express them, they should not have been published.

Another theme common to these cases was that controversial ideas were presented as science—as conclusions based on evidence. Critics argued that presenting one side of the issue as empirical fact gives it a special status in debate, rendering it more credible (for example Sheinin, 1993; Zimmerman, cited in Montagnes, 1993). A critic of Professor Freeman's article, Professor Cannie Stark, said: "If Freeman had actually conducted social research in a scientific manner ... if he had examined alternative explanations and weighed them in a dispassionate, scholarly fashion, if he had done all this and yet had been driven, by the force of the carefully gathered data, to similar conclusions, then we ... should be compelled to give his conclusions serious attention" (cited in Montagnes, 1993, p. 197). Science is a powerful trump card.

But if tagging an opinion as "science" gives it a special cachet, it also makes it vulnerable to attack on the grounds that it isn't *real* science. Professor Rushton's work was called "shoddy science"; the Rind et al. paper was called "junk science." Dr. Laura challenged the APA with regard to the sexual abuse paper: "If it's science, why don't they endorse it? If it isn't science, why do they publish it?" (quoted in Lilienfeld, 2002, p. 181).

Reflecting on events in the Rind et al. case, some social scientists have come up with suggestions for avoiding or mitigating such crises in future. These were summed up by Bennett Berenthal (2002), former assistant director of the Directorate of Social, Behavioral and Economic Sciences (SBE) at the National Science Foundation in the United States. He suggested that science organizations and researchers should be better prepared for the politicization of their work and recognize that research findings can be abused by those with various social and political agendas. Scientific organizations, some say, ought to seize every opportunity to educate policymakers, the news media, and the public about research, peer review, and controversies in science.

Deborah Phillips (2002), who worked at the National Academy of Sciences on the implications of social science research for public policy, recommends that authors, editors, and reviewers need to be more aware of, and comment on, the social significance of their findings. Discussion sections of scientific articles should comment on the findings and their implications for public policy. "Reviewers, many of whom may not be in a particularly good position to evaluate statements about policy or other broad implications of the results ... need explicit guidance about how to assess these commentaries during the editorial review process," she maintains (p. 220).

More Speech, Less Speech

Current thinking about how to deal with extremely unpopular ideas has focused on the notion of "more speech." Coleman and Alger (1996) came up with the term to counter the notion that some ideas should be censored because they stigmatize certain groups (such as Blacks in Rushton's evolutionary theory, or working mothers in Freeman's paper). More speech is designed to offset the potential marginalization of target groups by responding to or rebutting the stigmatizing viewpoint.

According to Coleman and Alger, the goal is to find a way to support marginalized groups while maintaining everyone's right to free speech. The ideal is a society that values both free expression and non-discrimination. Societies, institutions, and individuals can exercise their own free speech rights to disagree with or denounce attitudes or comments perceived to be objectionable.

Emphasizing more speech rather than censorship serves an educational purpose by exposing prejudice and prompting critical examination of stereotypes. Institutions such as universities, scientific organizations, and their like should ensure that competing voices are heard within the institution's programs, activities, and publications. Incoming APA president (and former *Psychological Bulletin* editor) Robert J. Sternberg (2002) has listed various ways in which editors can balance articles with more speech:

> A controversial article can be published along with one or more companion pieces that represent different perspectives or points of view that put the original piece in one or more alternative contexts. [Editors] can at least show that they recognize the sensitivity of the particular issue raised, while in no way banning or otherwise interfering with the publication of the original piece.
> An editor can choose to write an editorial that provides a larger context for the article. In this way, the editor sets the stage and recognizes the kinds of issues that may arise from the article.
> An editor can work with authors of an article to word things very carefully and, in general, to do everything possible to head off possible misinterpretation of what is being said. The goal here is not to change the message but rather to make clear exactly what that message is in the light of misunderstandings that are likely to arise. (p. 195–196)

Professor Sternberg's first two points are consistent with the more-speech notion. The third is aimed at clarifying the message. In the Rushton case, for example, the author has said that there is more differentiation within human groups than between them and that there is "a great deal of intraracial variability within each broad grouping" (1991, p. 29); in the Rind case, the authors noted that whatever their findings about the pathology resulting from adult-child sex, there are still legal and social reasons to consider such relationships to be wrong. In both cases, the authors did not highlight these qualifications or only did so when the controversies were already in full bloom (see Rushton, 1991; Rind et al., 2001).

The American Psychological Association eventually found its way out of the morass of the Rind et al. and Lilienfeld controversies by taking a more-speech approach. The flagship journal *American Psychologist*, which earlier had seemed to be opting for suppression with regard to the Lilienfeld article, produced a special issue in March 2002 with multiple perspectives from various sides of the issue. To the extent that this action refurbished the APA's reputation, the strategy is a testament to the value of the "more-speech" approach and a lesson in the failure of censorship.

According to Georges Minois (1995), it is a permanent paradox of censorship that it is always the strongest publicity agent for banned works. Coleman and Alger (1996) say that speech codes and other restrictions on expression serve only to repress manifestations of ignorance. When offensive opinions are hidden from view, the chance to correct them by astute counter-argument is lost.

Censorship and suppression give us "less speech." Thus, in the Freeman case, the National Research Council wanted to limit the debate so that Professor Freeman "would not have his day in Court." In the Rind et al. case, the American Psychological Association seemed ready to suppress the Lilienfeld article that would have exposed and commented upon many aspects of the controversy.

If we condone censorship, we can never be sure whether the grounds of suppression are what they are purported to be. Is it the method or is it the message? In the Lilienfeld controversy, to what extent was the re-review prompted by the author's criticism of the publisher, the APA? Often, censorship can be deconstructed so that explicit reasons are found to hide other reasons that are awkward to state (see Best, 2001).

The attempt to protect marginalized groups from offensive comments and conclusions is exemplified by a 1993 policy statement by the Ontario Ministry of Education and Training entitled "Framework Regarding Harassment and Discrimination in Ontario Universities and Colleges" (Horn, 1999). Harassment is defined as anything offensive, hostile, or inappropriate concerning gender, race, ethnicity, religion, sexual preference, or disability. Exclusionary rules apply to anything from speech containing jokes and taunts to books in libraries and art exhibitions.

In contrast to such speech-code approaches, the argument for more speech urges us to develop and promulgate as many ideas and opinions as possible about a range of topics and positions, some of which fly in the face of our deeply held beliefs, or even what we consider to be common sense. (Dr. Laura, in the Rind et al. controversy, said that any scientific findings that conflict with common sense should be regarded as erroneous [quoted in Lilienfeld, 2002]).

Some argue that controversial articles such as those described here would never appear in print if editors and reviewers did their jobs. Some point to apparent methodological problems or to perceived biases of the authors in order to make a case for less speech. On the other side of the argument, however, Rauch (1999) noted: "A lot of science is flawed, and most scientists have biases. The answer is for other scientists with other biases to do more science" (p. 2270).

Finally: Whose rights are at stake?

Ethicist Arthur Schafer (1989), commenting on the Rushton case, said, "We are committed to extend the right of freedom of expression to every point of view. This right includes publications that some find objectionable; those who are shocked or offended have an equal right to reply" (A7). Professor Schafer is clearly putting the case for more speech rather than censorship. But has he got the case for "rights" right?

Instead of asking what rights Professors Rushton, Freeman, and Rind have or ought to have, I submit that the real issue is what rights *we* have. The question is not whether all points of view have a right to be *heard*, but do we have a right to *hear* all points of view? Censorship and suppression are not only, and perhaps not even primarily, an assault on someone's right to be heard, but an assault on *our* right to hear the evidence, to weigh the arguments, and to make up our own minds.

2

September 11 and the Failures of American Intellectuals

Robert Jensen

In 1979 I worked as a busboy in a restaurant in one of the Washington, DC, suburbs, where I became friends with one of the dishwashers, who was Middle Eastern. On a slow night when I first got to know him, we sat for a long time talking, and I asked him what country he was from. "Persia," he said. I looked at him, confused. "I don't understand," I said. "Persia isn't a country anymore." He smiled and explained. He was Iranian. But this was after the fall of the Shah, when Americans from the US embassy in Tehran were being held in the infamous "hostage crisis." All over the United States, Iranians and Iranian-Americans were subject to both verbal and physical abuse. My restaurant friend explained that to avoid such abuse, he simply told Americans he was from Persia, and that took care of it. He said he felt bad about fudging his own nationality, but he was scared for his safety.

At the time, I was a temporary college dropout, with no particular expertise in the Middle East. But from the papers and my dim memories of world history class, I knew that modern-day Iran had taken the place of what had been called Persia. I couldn't have told anyone much about the history of the Persian Empire or contemporary Iranian politics beyond what was in the news at the time. But I had assumed everyone knew at least as much as I knew, which wasn't much. I asked him how he could fool people simply by calling himself Persian. He smiled.

"I don't mean to sound rude," he said. "But it's easy to fool Americans."

The Eggshell of Ignorance
The Buddha is said to have spoken of enlightenment as emerging from the eggshell of ignorance. The events of 9/11 shattered our eggshell and presented Americans with a stark choice. For too long we had lived with a willed ignorance about the consequences of US economic, foreign, and military policy. To many, ignorance felt like protection from the world—on the absurd assumption that what we don't know can't hurt us—but in reality it was always eggshell-thin.

This ignorance was perhaps most clearly expressed by the president of the United States. At an October 11, 2001, news conference, Bush told reporters he was amazed by what he called the "vitriolic hatred for America" in some Islamic countries. He explained:

> I'm amazed that there is such misunderstanding of what our country is about, that people would hate us. I am, I am—like most Americans, I just can't believe it. Because I know how good we are, and we've go to do a better job of making our case. We've got to do a better job of explaining to the people in the Middle East, for example, that we don't fight a war against Islam or Muslims. We don't hold any religion accountable. We're fighting evil. And these murderers have hijacked a great religion in order to justify their evil deeds. And we cannot let it stand.[1]

We should give the American public the benefit of the doubt and assume that most were not quite as amazed as the president. But Bush was not the only American who was inside the eggshell on September 10, 2001. On September 11, we had the opportunity to emerge, newly engaged in honest attempts to understand the world and our place in it. But many Americans desperately tried to paste the old eggshell back together. On this front, Bush also took the lead. On September

27, 2001, Bush appeared at O'Hare airport in Chicago and encouraged people to "get on board," but not with a serious plan for educating ourselves. His advice:

> When they struck, they wanted to create an atmosphere of fear. And one of the great goals of this nation's war is to restore public confidence in the airline industry. It's to tell the traveling public: Get on board. Do your business around the country. Fly and enjoy America's great destination spots. Get down to Disney World in Florida. Take your families and enjoy life, the way we want it to be enjoyed.[2]

So a president who claims not to understand what is obvious to virtually everyone outside the United States—that no matter what the twisted theology and ideology of Al Qaeda, lots of people in the Arab and Muslim world object to US foreign policy for perfectly rational reasons—suggests the appropriate responses are to:

1. explain to people in the Middle East why they don't understand American benevolence; and

2. explain to people in the United States that they should go to Disney World, a fantasy park where one can ignore reality.

The United States is a society where people not only get by without knowing much about the wider world but are systematically encouraged not to think independently or critically. Instead, Americans are urged to accept the myth of the United States as a benevolent, misunderstood giant lumbering around the world trying to do good. That means the crisis in which we find ourselves after 9/11 is not only political but intellectual, a problem not just of doing but of knowing.

Institutional Accountability

Part of the responsibility for this failure of knowing in American culture lies with the universities. This was true before 9/11, and even was more obvious after that day. Much to my sadness, US faculty members—conservative and liberal alike—have for the most part either actively encouraged the avoidance of unpleasant realities or failed to fulfill their obligation to guide people toward the knowledge that would help deconstruct American mythology. This failure becomes clear when we look at the main responses to 9/11 in the intellectual world. There were five basic positions staked out:

The Ultra-Hawks. These people started with the assumption that we had to respond to the attacks of 9/11 with massive military force, arguing that the United States is the benevolent empire and the empire should do its work. If you disagreed with that approach, you were a fool, a dupe, or a subversive.

The Hawks. This group conceded that there could be a debate about war so long as that debate distorted, trivialized, and marginalized arguments against war. There was no need to analyze the situation beyond clichés about "Islamic fascism" and the assertion that the power to bomb equals the right to bomb equals the inevitability of bombing equals the nobility of bombing. After this pseudo-debate was over (which was quickly), the only possible path was war.

The Cultural Doves. The focus of this group was the need to understand other cultures while avoiding the crucial political issues and abstaining from debate about war.

The Political Doves-with-Wings-Pinned. These folks generally said that bombing is bad policy but largely avoided doing anything to press that point or to confront directly the political culture's myth of American goodness lest they offend—as offending people is bad.

The Anti-Empire Crowd. People critiquing American foreign policy and militarism from an internationalist perspective rejected claims about American exceptionalism and engaged in public education and political organizing.

From that construction it is obvious I put myself in the last category (with the implication, of course, that it is the appropriate analysis and strategy). But here I am more interested in what we can learn about American intellectuals from the other four categories.

In certain intellectual and political circles, it is easy to criticize the Ultra-Hawks; their demand for a reflexive subordination to political leaders is a profoundly anti-intellectual position that inhibits critical thinking and democracy, which are inextricably linked. The Hawks are marginally more sophisticated in their approach, realizing that crude nationalism is not always effective. But in the end, there is little meaningful difference between the Ultra and Regular-Strength Hawks. Both groups ignore evidence and arguments that undermine their positions because the realities of power allow them to do so.

Perhaps that is why, a few weeks after 9/11, a Canadian Broadcasting Corporation radio producer who wanted to set up a debate between the anti- and pro-war positions called, saying she might have to cancel the segment because she couldn't find a pro-war faculty member in the United States to debate me on the air. I was incredulous and told her that I couldn't believe people were afraid of debating me (I'm not that formidable or well known). She agreed and said it had nothing to do with me. The pro-war folks she had talked to simply said they weren't interested in a debate—with anyone. Most likely their refusal was based on the assessment that they had already won. Why get mixed up in a public debate in which you would have to defend your views when your views have already prevailed?

But for all the obvious problems in these Hawk positions (assuming one believes that facts matter in determining a course of action and that moral considerations are relevant to policy discussions), one often can learn more from looking closely at the positions of what, at first glance, appear to be one's allies. I do not take this scrutiny to be a case of petty backbiting but rather important to an examination of fundamental flaws in US intellectual and political culture. My target is not a specific political position but the way in which US intellectuals have contributed to the depoliticization of the culture more generally.

The Cultural Doves are well-intentioned, which usually makes them dangerous. For example, after 9/11, many non-Muslims rushed to buy books on Islam. There's nothing wrong with wanting to know more about Islam, and a complete understanding of what happened on 9/11 involves some knowledge of Islam. But far more important for most Americans is expanding their knowledge about US foreign policy. That is, 9/11 involved theology, but it was primarily a political event, not a religious one. This tendency in the United States to want to explain things in cultural, not political, terms is dangerous in an already deeply depoliticized society.

We should never expect much, in terms of analysis or political action, from the Cultural Doves. I want to concentrate on the Political Doves-with-Wings-Pinned and try to bring into sharp focus some of the current intellectual and political problems I see with this position. To do this, I'm going to quote extensively from an e-mail exchange I had with a fellow professor—whom I'll call John here—at the University of Texas. John has always been thoughtful and engaged in his interactions with me and has tried, in his own way, to be supportive of my political work. He shares his own views with the public through op-ed writing, which I support, even though I rarely agree with the approach he takes in his writing. He is a serious scholar in his field, and I have no reason to think he is not a principled person. But even with all those endorsements, I think his approach to politics—and the connection between professional intellectuals and politics—exemplifies some of what is wrong with the US academy.

The Importance of Engaging

This e-mail exchange started after I had been publicly condemned by the president of the University of Texas for writing articles critical of the mad rush to war after 9/11. John was critical of the president's actions and of me.

John thought it untoward of me, in responding to criticism, to "act as if your piece was reasonable and inoffensive." The marriage of the two descriptions implies that reasoned arguments should be inoffensive. I think my writing was, and continues to be, reasonable—that is, I present accurate factual evidence, rational arguments, and a defensible conclusion. I also understand that it offends many people. It is hardly surprising that some very reasonable presentations are also very offensive to some. Anyone who has ever taught material that deals with political and social issues knows, for example, that students who hear a point of view that contradicts what they have long been taught—and believed—may well be offended; it's sometimes a sign that real learning is taking place.

John also suggested that I had "initiated an inflammatory argument" with my article, which I think gets the sequence of events wrong. The hawkish and inflammatory rhetoric of the Bush administration, members of Congress (both Republican and Democrat), TV anchors, pundits, and many others within the first hours after the attack "initiated" the argument and made it necessary for people with anti-war politics to respond immediately and decisively. I knew perfectly well that the piece I wrote would anger the majority of Americans. My goal at that moment was not to convince everyone that a war would be wrong; I knew that would be impossible. My goal was to reach out to progressive people who might be struggling for a way to understand the events of the day, to give them an analysis that would be otherwise hard to find in the mass media, to let them know they weren't alone. My e-mail traffic in the days, and months, after 9/11 suggests that I—and many others writing and speaking in similar fashion—accomplished that. I knew, however, that many people would be angry with me.

John's response was that I had admitted I "did not care about how the majority of people would react." Indeed, I not only knew many would be angry but didn't care, in moral terms (I cared in strategic terms but judged that the goal of reaching one segment of the US public outweighed the effects of angering another). I didn't care then, and I don't care now, because I believed—and continue to believe—that the lives of people outside the United States, which would be targeted in a US war, were more important than the feelings of people inside the United States. My intention was to help build an anti-war movement that could derail the expected US military response. If a successful movement could help save innocent lives, would that not trump concerns about offending or angering some Americans? In fact, would not one be morally obligated to offend Americans?

I am not succumbing to delusional self-aggrandizement. I did not somehow think my op-eds, radio interviews, or public talks would turn the tide, and I was not naïve about the chances of stopping the US attack on Afghanistan. But whatever the chances, the calculation that many in the anti-war movement made seems to me, in retrospect, to have been correct. One could argue that a less confrontational strategy could have been more effective (though I don't see any evi-

dence for it), but that's a tactical issue, not a question of principle.
But here is the most distressing thing John said to me:

> All I can say, Bob, AGAIN is that I am glad for you that you can view the world in such black and white terms, a world where Bob Jensen carries and promotes truth and virtue, and those who react to the things he does should be judged without considering what he has done to provoke such reactions, or what he might have done to make the outcome different.

In fact, I did consider the reactions my work could be expected to provoke, and I judged the potential negative reactions to be less important than the pursuit of what I believed—and still believe—was a compelling political goal that easily outweighs offending some. But to me the distressing part of the above paragraph is that John seems to take refuge in—and implicitly makes a virtue of—what he describes elsewhere as an inability or unwillingness to form a clear conclusion on which one can act; he denigrates my attempt to do the opposite. In his formulation, I am reduced to a simplistic thinker who can see only black and white, apparently less virtuous than those who see the many shades of gray.

I have never claimed to be a big thinker or an important theorist. I consider myself a competent, hard-working, second-tier intellectual. I have never broken new ground, but I can do reasonably decent work building on the insights of others. I am far from the most sophisticated thinker in the world, but I think I have mastered the basics of informal logic and argumentation. And I realize the world is a complex place. But no matter what the complexity of the world, we have moral obligations that don't go away simply because we might not be absolutely certain about the causes and consequences of actions in that complex world. One of the tasks of an intellectual should be to look for patterns in the world's complexity that can guide us in making moral and political decisions. The importance of that task increases dramatically when one lives in the most powerful country in the history of the planet, a country in which leaders have demonstrated repeatedly a willingness to use horrific levels of violence to impose their will on others.

I do not see the world in black and white. The shades of gray bedevil me as much as the next person. Like most people, I live with high levels of self-doubt. But I do not think those shadings absolve me of my responsibility. We should approach that responsibility with great humility and openness to counter-arguments; we should always keep in mind that we act with imperfect knowledge. History reminds us that no small number of people who acted out of certainty about the accuracy of their analyses and the righteousness of their moral stances have brought upon the innocents of the world suffering beyond description.

It is also true that I live in a country that drops cluster bombs in civilian areas. I have never lived anywhere that was the target of a cluster bomb, but I suspect that when a cluster bomb detonates above a person and its couple of hundred individual bomblets are dispersed to do their flesh-shredding work, the world looks pretty black and white. I suspect that when one sees a child pick up an unexploded bomblet, which then explodes and rips off the child's head, the world looks pretty black and white. Should the world look any less black and white when one lives in the country that drops those bombs? When the chairman of the Joint Chiefs of Staff explains, in response to a question of why such a weapon is used, "We only use cluster munitions when they are the most effective weapon for the intended target,"[3] how long can we allow ourselves to paint pictures with the many shades of gray?

What a Healthy Intellectual Community Would Look Like

Right after 9/11 there was a spate of stories about the pressures faced by faculty members who didn't fall in line behind the so-called war on terrorism. But, with rare exceptions, those pressures were informal or social, not formal or legal. For example, I know of no direct action taken by administrators at the University of Texas, where I work, to silence dissent.

My critique of universities is not that administrators routinely persecuted dissidents, just as my criticism of most academics is not that they didn't agree with me. Instead, the fundamental failure of US universities after 9/11 was their unwillingness to take seriously their role as centres of knowledge and their refusal to create space for debate and discussion. If American campuses were healthy intellectual communities, after 9/11 they would have been hotbeds of discussion.

People often ask me, what would you have done if you had been president of your university? The answer is simple: After 9/11, I would have reserved the largest hall on campus for a weekly series of programs on terrorism and American foreign policy, drawing on the expertise of the campus from as many perspectives as possible. I would have committed resources from my office to publicize the forums as widely as possible. I would have made it clear that the university saw the enhancement of public discussion as central to its mission. I would have explained that while the university as an institution would take no specific position on policy choices, it would facilitate the broadest and deepest discussion possible. I would have asked my staff to work with the local television and radio stations, especially cable access TV and community radio, to broadcast these forums. And I would have encouraged faculty members to take up these issues in the classroom when relevant.

In short, I would have taken seriously the notion that the university is a place where citizens can expect to find information, analysis, and engagement. I would have realized that at such a pivotal moment in the nation's history, the university had a unique role to play. But the University of Texas did none of that, nor did most universities in the United States. At some universities, small groups of faculty who were concerned about the direction the country was heading did their best to create such space. But on most campuses, a tiny minority of faculty was involved in such efforts, and an even smaller minority of administrators aided them. Many of the events on campuses were student organized, efforts that were important and admirable. But it's a shame that, in most cases, university officials and faculty members chose to duck and cover.

A Problem of the University, and Beyond

Why would the largest university in the country, with such tremendous human and material resources, be so politically disengaged at such a crucial time? No doubt part of the explanation for the timid performance of the University of Texas, and institutions of higher education more generally, is specific to that moment. The United States had never experienced an attack on its civilian population of the magnitude of 9/11, and it's easy to understand why many people lost their voices in the highly emotional, hyperpatriotic fervor that followed. But college campuses have not been centres of critical inquiry in some time (and even when they were, as in the 1960s, much of the most vibrant intellectual and political activity was student led). Although I won't pretend that there was ever in the United States a golden age when universities were completely free spaces, a contributing factor to this consistent failure is intensifying economic pressures as public universities are forced to find more and more funding from private sources and an ethic of public service continues to wither.[4] Faculty feel this pressure, which subtly encourages professors to act not as members of a community of scholars with obligations to the public but as independent agents with the goal of maximizing grant funding and personal status. The market model dominates not only the organization of the institution but the mission as well, as students increasingly look at a university education not as an opportunity for intellectual enrichment but a ticket to upward mobility and career advancement.

But there also is a larger lesson about the state of American political culture in all of this. I quoted extensively from my exchange with John because he is one of the professors on campus who routinely offers his views on matters of public concern to the public. He and I agree that academics should be part of the political dialogue not just in the classroom or with scholarly colleagues but in the larger world as well. But also in his comments are, I believe, strains of a view common in the United States: If one talks politics, one should make sure others are not offended. The often-repeated advice is that it's best to avoid talking politics or religion at the dinner table (or at social gatherings in general), but I don't think that advice captures the real rule in the contemporary United States: One may talk politics or religion as long as it doesn't upset anyone. In my limited travels abroad and extensive discussions with people from other countries, this practice appears to be peculiar to Americans (and especially to white middle-class Americans).

At the heart of this play-nice/avoid-conflict/make-sure-no-one-feels-uncomfortable style is an implicit abandonment of both intellectual standards and political life. If we can't engage each other and take the chance that tempers might flare, then we will be less likely to subject each other's arguments to critical scrutiny. And if we don't routinely involve ourselves in those kinds of exchanges, the skills of informal logic and argumentation—the ability to identify the logical path of a claim and evaluate the evidence—will atrophy. Yes, it's true that political debate sometimes descends into name calling and emotional outbursts that can be destructive or even abusive. But that's all the more reason for those who have claims based in logic and evidence to be willing to debate—with passion—those claims. If argumentation (of the rigorous kind) is not going to degrade into mere argument (of the inane kind), we all have to be willing to engage with each other.

Degraded arguments were around before 9/11. Here's an earlier example: When the US attack on Yugoslavia began in 1999, I posted a message to a progressive faculty e-mail list about a local demonstration against the bombing. One member of the list responded, asking if this were perhaps a case where progressive people should be supporting a US war. Because I knew a lot of folks were buying Clinton's "humanitarian intervention" argument, I wrote a response that explained why I believed US actions were humanitarian in neither motivation nor effect, and why one should oppose the policy as immoral and illegal. My response politely but firmly put forward a political argument, not a personal attack; I made no reference to the person who had written, only to the political position she had articulated. But another list member posted a note accusing me of just such a personal attack and cautioning against such posts. I was a bit taken aback; even in an allegedly left circle, and among other university faculty, I was being chastised for arguing forcefully for a position when someone else in the group took a different position. One other person on the e-mail list defended the need for such exchanges of views, but the list generally fell silent, rendering useless a possible site for discussion and organizing. I have no idea what kept people from talking or getting involved, though I assumed part of the answer involved a fear of venturing into territory where there would be sharp disagreement.

Disciplining Dissent

Is it too much to ask that people—especially faculty at a public university—be willing to engage in the spirited intellectual and political exchanges that should be the lifeblood of a healthy democracy? We cannot simply blame politicians or loud-mouthed TV talk-show hosts for the sad state of our political culture and feel absolved. We have to take responsibility ourselves.

Part II
Corporate Takeovers: Case Studies

3

You Have No Right to Present This Research

David Healy

Behind the Veneer of Science

November 2000

I had never bought a copy of *Forbes* in my life, but the November 27, 2000, issue, whose front cover depicted a strangely Muslim-looking figure under the banner headline "Corporate Saboteurs," was irresistible. The cover line read: "They wrecked Monsanto. Now they're after the US Drug Industry. Is your company next?" A disappointingly superficial article inside charted the rise of the anti-capitalist and anti-globalization demonstrations that had been such a feature of the news in 2000 and 2001 (Lenzner & Kellner, 2000). But it was the conjunction of an apparently Muslim figure on the cover and a first hint that Big Pharma might feel itself to be under threat that drew my attention. No one could have guessed that this was just about the right date for a conception that would lead to a birth nine months later. This birth would fuse the war of civilizations some social commentators seemed to be talking up and the discontents surrounding globalization.

At the time, I knew nothing of the work of Sheldon Rampton and John Stauber, both of the Center for Media and Democracy, who a few years earlier had charted a new world that made sense of the *Forbes* front cover. Stauber and Rampton (1995) had outlined a world where corporations avoided facing off against their radical critics (as they had done in the 1960s), by penetrating these very groups, offering consultancies to these critics, or setting up alternative ecological or consumer groups. This new world was one where companies retained "independent" experts to offer rapid responses to adverse stories in the media. It was common knowledge that Big Tobacco had been doing something like this, but as Stauber and Rampton made clear, the practice had become the norm for all corporations. We had slipped into a world in which scientific data, or the spin put on scientific data, could be used to prove anything—even that toxic sludge was good for you.

This work was developed further by Rampton and Stauber (2001) and independently by Thomas Frank (2000), but none of it has much, if any, resonance within psychiatry today. Completely unaware of connections to this body of work, I was due to speak on some of these very same issues three days later at a meeting at the University of Toronto. At the time, I was contracted to move from the United Kingdom to the University of Toronto Department of Psychiatry, and while waiting for the final stages of the visa application process to run their course, I had been invited to give a lecture at a meeting to celebrate the 75th anniversary of the university department and the 150th anniversary of the Queen Street Mental Health Facility.

It may seem odd that the work of Stauber and Rampton has little or no resonance within psychiatry, which is commonly seen as the most socially aware branch of medicine. The history of the discipline supports perceptions of its social connectedness. Many of the signatories of the documents that inaugurated the French Revolution were also members of Franz Mesmer's Society of Harmony; their work with early forms of hypnosis had led to some of the first perceptions that the entire social order might be held in place by suggestion and could be radically refashioned (Healy, 1993). It is no accident that one of the abiding images of the French Revolution is Philippe Pinel's liberation of the insane from their shackles.

The social processes that the French Revolution inaugurated arguably came to their climax in the mid-1960s, when a new world was born. In that new world, the hegemony of white middle-aged and middle-class men was overthrown and women, ethnic groups, the young, and others claimed a place in the government of us all. The social revolutions of the 1960s were shaped heavily by psychiatrists. Laing, Goffman, Fanon, Marcuse, Foucault, and Szasz were all either psychiatrists or philosophers or sociologists who adopted a psychiatric metaphor for the ills of society, creating in the process what came to be called "antipsychiatry" (Healy, 2002). The antipsychiatrists claimed that madness was a myth used by society to control dissidence.

But if there is something about psychiatry that connects it to major world events, there is something else about it that has most of the profession swinging from engagement with the world at one moment to almost complete disengagement at the next. Following Mesmer, psychiatry conspired in the banning of hypnosis/psychotherapy for almost a century. Following Pinel, psychiatrists incarcerated themselves in asylums. My talk in Toronto was concerned with what happened to us following the turmoil of antipsychiatry. My argument was that orthodox psychiatry had not overcome antipsychiatry but rather both had been subsumed by a new corporate psychiatry.

I presented the story on November 30, 2000, as a rather fresh-faced historian of psychopharmacology, who, after digging into the primary sources, had a story to tell about a dog that had barked furiously in the 1960s and had since been silenced. There was a certain drama to the story that seemed to restore some excitement to psychiatry. It was a story told at what I thought was a relatively abstract take-it-or-leave-it level. It glancingly touched upon the fact that companies now regularly set up patient groups, and that an increasing proportion of the scientific literature in psychopharmacology is ghost-written. This level allowed audience members to congratulate themselves on being involved in an exciting discipline and yet leave the meeting without feeling any need to change their practices. Almost immediately after giving this lecture, however, I learned the university had breached my contract.

Against the background outlined above, perhaps the only surprise about my contract being breached was the level of surprise at the event. It was conceivable that something like this could happen, yet astonishing when it did. But if the background retrospectively makes it clear an accident was waiting to happen, the combination of events nevertheless warrants attention.

September 2000
The September issue of *The Economics of Neuroscience* (*TEN*), a glossy magazine with some of the appearances of a scientific psychiatric journal, including a large number of advertisements for psychotropic drugs, featured a front cover showing Charles Nemeroff with a sidebar stating: "Boss of Bosses. Is the brash and controversial Charles Nemeroff the most powerful man in psychiatry?"

A few months previous in July 2000, at a British Association for Psychopharmacology (BAP) meeting, I had presented the results of a study done with colleagues, which involved giving either sertraline or reboxetine to healthy volunteers. The prior personalities of the volunteers appeared to predict who would be suited to which drug—one acted on the serotonin system (sertraline) and one didn't (Tranter et al., 2002). In the case of sertraline, two of our volunteers became suicidal (Healy, 2000a). These data overlapped with data obtained by pharmaceutical companies developing selective serotonin reuptake inhibitor (SSRI) drugs. They had given these drugs to healthy volunteers during the mid-1980s as part of the development process.

Dr. Nemeroff was a guest lecturer at this BAP meeting. In a private conversation, he told me I had no right to present these data. That it would be the end of my career. That he had been approached to get involved in legal actions against me. A few weeks later I was invited to speak at the Toronto meeting, where, I soon learned, Dr. Nemeroff was also due to be a speaker.

At the time I didn't know that Chamberlain Communications Group, a New York public relations group working for pharmaceutical company Eli Lilly, was involved in preparing the ground for the launch of a derivative of Lilly's SSRI antidepressant, Prozac. It seems that among the marketplace obstacles Chamberlain had scheduled for management were Joseph Glenmullen and David Healy.

Joseph Glenmullen is the author of *Prozac Backlash*, which had been published in April 2000 (Glenmullen 2000). A series of reviews of this book—apparently authored by such senior figures in US psychiatry as Rothschild, Dunner, Greist, Ruben, and Emslie—were sent to many media outlets shortly afterwards. These reviews had a consistent theme, which from the start has been at the heart of Lilly's defence of Prozac against claims that it can trigger suicidality: namely, that Prozac is one of the most-researched drugs in history and any problems of suicidality stem from the disease, depression, and not its treatment with Prozac. The supposed great tragedy of cautionary books like *Prozac Backlash* is that patients who are at risk of committing suicide will be scared away from effective treatment and, as a result, will end up committing suicide.

A set of reviews went to Jamie Talan of *Newsday* in New York with a covering letter from Robert Schwadron of Chamberlain Communications. In his covering letter, Schwadron offered to arrange for interviews about *Prozac Backlash* with members of Eli Lilly as well as independent researchers from the medical community. Schwadron's letter was sent on notepaper with Chamberlain's logo, which features a target. These reviews offer convincing evidence of how Chamberlain had targeted Dr. Glenmullen.

In my case, the views I had expressed at my lecture in Toronto were entirely consistent with views expressed two years before in *The Antidepressant Era* (Healy, 1998). This book does not detail any side effects of psychotropic drugs and is not hostile to industry, although it does outline the growing power of pharmaceutical companies within the therapeutic marketplace. It was reviewed favourably by clinicians as well as investigators and others working with the pharmaceutical industry. Yet, a few years later, these same views were being described as "controversial." Colleagues phoned from Canada, the United States, Japan, and elsewhere to warn me that I was being described as "trouble." These descriptions all appeared to originate with US psychiatrists, who neither knew me nor had heard me talk but seemed convinced that I was trying to damage the pharmaceutical industry.

In April 2000, views comparable to those in *The Antidepressant Era* and my Toronto talk but specific to Prozac had been published as one of a series of five articles on Prozac in the Spring 2000 issue of the *Hastings Center Report* (Healy, 2000b). This article led Lilly, who at that time I understood to be one of the single biggest funders of the

Hastings Center, to pull their funding from the center.

There might appear to be a smoking gun leading back to Lilly. However, the day after the Toronto lecture, I was due to visit the archives of Pfizer, the makers of sertraline, in New York as part of a legal action. Pfizer knew that one of things I was likely to find was evidence of a healthy volunteer study it had conducted nearly twenty years before showing that its SSRI antidepressant, sertraline, had the potential to make healthy volunteers suicidal. Furthermore, I was also due to be an expert witness in a legal case against GlaxoSmithKline in Cheyenne, Wyoming, brought by a man whose father-in-law, a man in his early sixties, had been on Glaxo's paroxetine, another SSRI drug. After taking the drug for two days, the man killed his wife, daughter, and granddaughter before killing himself.

The only difference between 1998 and 2000 was my involvement in legal actions as an expert witness for the plaintiffs. This participation had come about because US legal firms apparently found it all but impossible to get experts to testify against pharmaceutical companies in actions involving the adverse effects of SSRI drugs.

Aside from the concerns US experts had for their research funds if they were seen to dissent from the pharmaceutical company line, there also appeared to be a genuine worry about the consequences at a personal level, consequences that my case now exemplifies. But there was another factor that led to a silencing of dissent. It was difficult to make a case against companies—not because there wasn't good evidence that the drugs could cause problems, but because of a consensus that had been manufactured.

Manufacturing Consensus

In the *TEN* profile, Dr. Nemeroff was cited as having a small and influential group of close friends including Alan Schatzberg, Martin Keller, and others. An example of how influential and connected such a network might be lies in Schatzberg and Nemeroff's 1998 *American Psychiatric Press Textbook of Psychopharmacology*, in which the chapter on SSRIs was written by Tollefson, an employee of the Lilly pharmaceutical company, and Rosenbaum from Massachusetts General Hospital, who had regularly written pieces defending Lilly and Prozac and had criticized *Prozac Backlash*. This chapter cited a study by Warshaw and Keller as its only piece of evidence that Prozac does not cause suicide. Any college student can ascertain that the Warshaw and Keller study was not designed to test whether Prozac could cause suicide. In fact, the only suicide in the study was committed by a subject taking Prozac.

Later, in a legal action taken against it for sertraline-induced suicide, Pfizer used this same chapter as evidence of certain "undisputed facts": that serotonin was low in depression; that SSRIs promote serotonergic function; and the selectivity of SSRIs makes them less likely than other antidepressants to have side effects. The consensus view, Pfizer claimed, made any action against companies regarding the hazards of SSRIs scientifically illegitimate. There is, however, no evidence for any lowering of serotonin in depression. The idea that there is such a lowering is marketing copy rather than evidence rooted in scientific data. The idea that SSRIs are freer of side effects than other antidepressants sits at odds with the almost complete failure of companies to publish collected quality-of-life data on these drugs. As regards triggering suicidality, the evidence that this group of drugs may do so is possibly stronger than any evidence for any major side effect of a currently used group of drugs—at least within psychiatry (Healy, 2003a).

The Role of Authorship in Consensus Building
Against this background consider the following e-mail: "Dear David, I am delighted you are able to participate in our satellite symposium.... In order to reduce your workload to a minimum we have had our ghost-writers produce a first draft based on your published work. I attach it here..."

The article that accompanied the e-mail was a recognizably Healy article, complete with Healy references saying the kinds of things I often say. Many people who think they know my work would probably be hard pressed to pick it out as a dud article.

However, before agreeing to get involved in this symposium in London, I had already mapped out what it was I wanted to say in the article I knew would have to be written. I sent a draft article back to the company, which was rather happy with the contents but made it clear that there were some commercially important points in the previous manuscript and that it would arrange for someone else to author that piece. The article I authored finally appeared in a journal supplement (Healy, 1999) beside the article that had been authored for me, with only one change as far as I could make out: the name of the author (Kasper, 1999).

Consider another example: An editorial in *The Lancet* examined how tainted medicine had become (*Lancet*, 2002). As an example of the taint, the editorial mentioned the publication of an article by Thase et al. (2001) on the merits of the SSRI antidepressant venlafaxine (Efexor) in the *British Journal of Psychiatry*, whose editor *The Lancet* claimed was a consultant to Wyeth.

The Thase article formed the basis of a campaign by Wyeth to try to persuade prescribers that while other SSRIs will help a certain proportion of people to get better, venlafaxine, Wyeth's drug, will do more—it will push people beyond better to well. The clinical trial data behind this claim were presented at a meeting held in Laguna Beach, California, in spring 2001. This meeting came complete with travel and accommodation expenses and honoraria, and offered participants at the meeting the opportunity to have their contributions written for them.

The communication from the medical-writing agency working for Wyeth, which brought a contribution to both me and a colleague, Richard Tranter, made it clear that we were free to edit the article in any way we chose. We edited it in two ways. One was to point out that clinical trial data for mirtazapine, a product competing directly with Wyeth's venlafaxine, appeared to give a message very different from the glowing one Wyeth was hoping to get across. Despite having been told that we were free to edit the original article in whatever way we chose, almost by return of e-mail there was an objection to the mention of mirtazapine.

A second point mentioned was the considerable evidence from clinical trials in both patients and healthy volunteers that individuals may or may not be suited to an SSRI. Personality types may in fact predict suitability to selective agents such as SSRIs. The same can be expected to hold true for venlafaxine—that is, if patients are not suited to venlafaxine, it will not get them either better or well but might, in fact, make them suicidal.

I did not attend the Laguna Beach meeting. The next time I saw the article it had already been sent to a Canadian journal, the *Journal of Psychiatry and Clinical Neuroscience*, which was going to publish the proceedings of the symposium. The final article had been revised extensively. Our reference to the fact that failing to match venlafaxine to patient could lead to problems including suicidality was missing.

There was also a new ending. Our original piece concluded that further research was needed. The new ending stated fairly explicitly that while further research was needed, in the meantime the best bet was to treat patients with venlafaxine. I objected to this claim and removed my name from the article.

Neither Wyeth nor the medical-writing agency had made the final set of changes; they had seemingly been coordinated by the University of Toronto's academic organizer for this meeting (Tranter et al., 2002b).

What these examples show is that the ghost-writing of "scientific articles" is commonplace and that industry is plainly wrong to say authors always have a chance to sign off on what is written. Critics of ghost-writing hitherto have regarded the problem as peripheral to the main concerns of science. In the 1980s, pharmaceutical companies outsourced much of their medical writing to medical-writing agencies. Companies also began setting up satellite symposia in conjunction with formerly scientific meetings. Journals began to publish the proceedings of satellite symposia in supplements. Until quite recently the assumption has been that ghost-writing is confined to review articles that appear primarily in journal supplements or obscure journals. The two articles listed above, some would argue, fall into these two categories. The problem, however, runs much deeper.

Current Medical Directions
Current Medical Directions (CMD) is a writing agency based in New York. Its mission statement says that CMD is a medical information company set up in 1990 "to deliver scientifically accurate information strategically developed for specific target audiences" (www.cmdconnect.com). This agency writes up studies, review articles, abstracts, journal supplements, product monographs, expert commentaries, and

textbook chapters. It conducts meta-analyses and organizes journal supplements, satellite symposia, and consensus conferences as well as advisory boards for its clients. In these endeavours the company "strives to exceed the expectations of our clients and to assist them in achieving their strategic objectives."

As of 1998, CMD was coordinating articles on Zoloft (sertraline), Pfizer's SSRI drug. A document outlining the articles being coordinated by CMD makes it clear that in the case of pieces on post-traumatic stress disorder (PTSD), first drafts of the articles were already prepared, and it appears that the writing agency was Paladin. The authors' names were listed TBD (to be determined) (CMD, 1999). In total, there were eighty-five articles being worked on, of which fifty-five had appeared by early 2001.

There is no way to know just exactly who wrote this set of articles, but the CMD document does define a set of articles on Zoloft. Along with a colleague, Dinah Cattell, I compared CMD and non-CMD articles systematically in three areas. First, we searched out all CMD and non-CMD articles and established the number of Medline citations attributed to each of the article's authors. Second, we established the impact factor of all journals in which all articles appeared. Third, we determined the subsequent citation rate of all articles.

A comparison reveals that the articles on Zoloft being coordinated by CMD appear in the journals with the highest impact factors in the field, including *JAMA*, the *American Journal of Psychiatry*, *Archives of General Psychiatry*, the *British Medical Journal*, and others. The authors of CMD articles are among the most highly Medline-cited authors in the field, with upward of 200 other articles per author. In brief, CMD articles appear in journals with an impact factor that is three times greater than the journals in which non-CMD articles appear. The CMD authors have a citation rate that is three times greater than non-CMD authors. And finally, the CMD articles end up being cited at a rate that is three times greater than the non-CMD articles.

It is of interest to find that the author's name most frequently found on these articles is Martin Keller of Brown University, Rhode Island. In 1998, the *Boston Globe* ran an article on Dr. Keller suggesting that he had earned over $800,000 from his links to pharmaceutical companies (Bass, 1999). One of the next most frequently represented authors on this list of CMD articles is Michael Thase.

There are a number of important points that stem from a consideration of this material. First, it makes clear that ghost-writing is not happening in peripheral journals, affecting review articles only. It probably happens in the most prestigious journals in medicine, and it probably happens as much, if not more often, for randomized trials and other data-driven papers as for review articles.

Second, the CMD articles exclusively cover areas of marketing concern for Pfizer. They are clinical trials or reviews of areas in which Pfizer had a marketing indication, such as depression, or in which it was then seeking one, such as PTSD. The published articles were not scientific studies designed to answer, for example, the question of which patients are best suited to an SSRI. These were not articles addressing scientific questions. These articles should be seen as manufacturing a consensus; if they deal with the hazards of treatment, they do so in order to put them "in context."

Third, as regards the context for hazards, there is a significant set of discrepancies between the CMD articles and the raw data underlying them. For instance, the CMD collection contains six Zoloft articles in which Zoloft was given in trials to children with obsessive-compulsive disorder or depression. One of these articles, which later appeared in *JAMA,* mentions one child becoming suicidal. Another article appearing in the *Journal of the American Academy of Child and Adolescent Psychiatry* states that the apparent authors are reporting on the side effects that had occurred at a 10 percent rate or more (Alderman et al., 1998). In fact, children who were depressed and went on Zoloft in this series of trials became suicidal at a 9 percent rate.

In another article appearing in the *British Medical Journal,* Malt and colleagues (1999) report on a study in which sertraline is compared with mianserin and placebo. Early drafts of the article mention that there is one suicide and three suicide attempts on sertraline, one suicide attempt on mianserin, and no suicide attempts of any sort on placebo. The final version does not mention any of these adverse effects.

There is good evidence that when it comes to suicidal acts in the clinical trials submitted to regulators who licence SSRIs such as Zoloft,

Prozac, and Paxil, the companies coded under the heading of placebo a significant number of suicidal acts that had actually not occurred. Without such manoeuvres, the data on a number of these drugs individually, and on the group as a whole, show that SSRIs trigger suicidality (Healy, 2003b). These manipulated data, in turn, have ended up in mainstream publications (Lopez-Ibor, 1993; Montgomery et al., 1995), and companies have appealed to this scientific data by apparently independent experts in the course of legal actions.

From the CMD data it is possible to conclude that up to 50 percent of the articles on therapeutics appearing in major journals are now ghost-written, and in the process important data on the hazards of therapy are being omitted or "put in context" (Healy & Cattell, 2003). But another aspect of this new scientific marketplace is that quite apart from the harassment of critics, there appears to be an active promotion of a consensus that favours industrial interests, which this also makes dissent increasingly difficult. Where before critics of a dominant scientific paradigm faced the inertia of a scientific establishment, they now face a consensus that is actively managed by public relations and medical-writing agencies in a manner that would have been inconceivable to Thomas Kuhn when he was writing *The Structure of Scientific Revolutions*.

There has been increasing media concern about the free meals and accommodation clinicians receive in ritzy hotels like the Waldorf and the educational meetings convened in the Caribbean or other comparable locations. Clinicians typically see the free pens, notepads, and mugs, as well as the meals and hotel rooms, as part of the marketing efforts of pharmaceutical companies, and they say they are not influenced by such factors. They claim they are only influenced by evidence and adhere to the evidence-based consensus on issues in the field. They fail to recognize that these trinkets and junkets are part of the gimmickry that stems from the sales rather than the marketing department of companies. The key work of the marketing department, in contrast, will often have been done before a drug is launched—that is, determining what clinical trials will be done for what therapeutic indications and appearing in which journals with which lead authors. The work of the marketing departments is to create "evidence" and establish consensus.

The CMD studies appear to be one result of this process. This is not a scientific literature aimed at addressing scientific questions. It is a set of infomercials that have the appearance of scientific articles. The literature is influential because of this appearance and because it is published under the names of some of the best-known clinical figures in the field in the most distinguished journals.

Risk Societies

In October 2002, *Newsweek* ran a cover piece on teenage depression (*Newsweek*, 2002) following trials run by Pfizer and GlaxoSmithKline on teenagers who were depressed. Until recently, no SSRIs had a licence for the treatment of nervous problems such as depression in children or adolescents.

Before these trials, clinicians did not need clinical studies conducted by Pfizer or Glaxo in order to treat children with SSRIs if this course seemed to be clinically indicated. A trial run by either Pfizer or Glaxo might have produced evidence that the drugs do not work in children in the way expected based on extrapolation from the adult data. Alternatively, if there were full disclosure of all data, such trials might have provided evidence of hazards in children not present in adults to the same extent.

In practice, however, running clinical trials gives Pfizer or Glaxo the opportunity to seek a licence for the treatment of children or adolescents with "depressive disorders." In fact, this is a licence to market the drug vigorously to these age groups: it is a licence to medicalize childhood and teenage misery.

Part of the medicalization will involve claims that childhood depression can lead to suicide and it is very important that this condition be detected and treated in order to reduce the risk of suicide. For clinicians practising according to the public evidence, however, there is a problem. As mentioned in Pfizer's trial of sertraline in depressed children, there was a 9 percent suicide attempt rate, but the published literature gives no hint of this finding. There are similar published and unpublished findings from GlaxoSmithKline's trials of a much-greater-than-placebo rate of suicidal acts for subjects on paroxetine (Keller et al., 2001).

Around 1990, the American Psychiatric Association and the British

College of Psychiatrists launched "defeat depression" campaigns. These campaigns were supported by money from pharmaceutical companies such as Eli Lilly and were extremely successful in converting cases of Valium, Librium, and Ativan into cases of Prozac, Paxil/Seroxat, and Zoloft/Lustral in the 1990s. A great part of the rhetoric of these campaigns centred on claims that the recognition of depression was extremely important so that this condition, which carried a high risk of suicide, could be treated effectively. Recognition and treatment would supposedly contribute to lowering national suicide rates, even though cases of Valium and Ativan had never been thought to be at much risk of suicide.

Unbeknownst to any of the psychiatrists involved in these campaigns and long before there was any public controversy about Prozac and its risk of triggering suicidality, data from SSRI trials for suicides and suicidal acts lodged with the Food and Drug Administration (FDA) in the US and the Medicines Control Agency (MCA) in Britain demonstrated that SSRIs could not, in principle, and at least without the proper warnings, lower suicide rates. These data make it clear that there is in fact a statistically significant increased risk of both suicides and suicidal acts in those on SSRI drugs (Healy, 2003a).

This story contains a message that goes beyond pointing out indicators of the degree to which psychiatrists can be duped. The key point lies in the potency of risk management as a sales technique. This strategy overlaps with claims from sociology that we now live in Risk Societies rather than class-based or ethnically based societies, that today what is distributed is not wealth so much as risk (Adam et al., 2000). The changing worldview involved can perhaps be seen most concretely in health care and reaches its clearest focus in mental health care. The first services in this domain were mental illness services, which became mental health services in the 1960s. Now, in the new millennium, they are fast becoming mental risk services. These changes are happening in tandem with changes in corporate strategies.

One of the key messages in *The Antidepressant Era* (Healy, 1998) is that companies no longer sell only medications but are as likely to sell diseases. In psychiatry this trend encouraged Pfizer to seek a licence for PTSD and teenage depression and its selling these concepts rather than sertraline with the expectation that sales of its drug will follow. This pattern of selling diseases can be seen in the marketing of osteoporosis, which leads to sales of hormone replacement therapy or calcium-enhancing drugs (Berman, 1999). It can be seen in the marketing of elevated lipid levels, which leads to the use of lipid-lowering drugs; the marketing of erectile dysfunction which leads to the use of sildenafil (Viagra); or, more recently, the marketing of bipolar disorder by a range of different companies, especially Lilly, which leads to the use of so-called mood stabilizers.

But there is another marketing double-step here. Where companies once produced medications for old-style diseases such as infections, they now produce medications that target risk factors such as elevated blood pressure, bone thinning, or the discontent that might lead to suicide.

The significance of this campaign lies in the size of the markets that open up. People with severe hypertension that poses a real risk of strokes or other disorders comprise a relatively small market. The number of women who actually break hips is again comparatively small. The number of people who commit suicide is 1 in 10,000. The number of all thirteen-year-old males who committed suicide in 1998 in the United States was thirty-one.

But the number of people who can be considered at risk for strokes, fractures of the hip, or suicide is very large. If one in ten who are at risk actually get the disorder, the traditional medical approach would lead to one in ten being treated. In contrast, a focus on risk management would lead to all ten being treated. In the case of teenagers who are depressed in the United States, *Newsweek* put the figure at 3 million.

This focus on risk management is of huge significance to companies who need to produce blockbuster drugs in order to survive. These are drugs that earn US$1.5 billion or more per year. Conventional medications simply won't earn this much. For some time it has been common knowledge that companies no longer develop drugs for real illnesses in the Third World owing to the lack of return on such products. But less well realized is that it is no longer economical for them to produce drugs for many major illnesses in the West unless these drugs can be sold off-licence for other indications.

The money is in blockbuster drugs. A very few of these are drugs like Viagra, which appear to be useful for what are thought of as "lifestyle options" rather than traditional diseases. The majority are drugs that act on risk factors rather than on core diseases.

Managing risk factors appeals to pharmaceutical companies for two reasons. One has to do with "quality." From an industrial point of view, a quality product is reliable in the sense that each unit is the same or delivers the same outcome each time. The Big Mac hamburger is the exemplar of a quality product. In contrast to treating actual diseases, where outcomes are always uncertain, risk factors such as elevated blood pressure or lipid levels can be reliably altered by drugs. This reliability offers industry an irresistible quality argument, even though reliably altering these risk factors may do little to affect a disease process that may or may not be present.

The second reason is that treating risk factors clearly offers a much larger market than treating diseases. But in addition to treating the pool of patients at serious risk from a disorder, risk thresholds can be ratcheted down progressively, creating ever-larger markets.

The problem for patients and for physicians is that they are rarely in possession of the figures that would let them make a balanced judgement about risks. For example, if either the patient or the physician knew that eight hundred people might have to be treated with an antihypertensive in order for that drug to save one life, it might influence a decision to take or prescribe a drug that might wipe out the patient's sex life or otherwise significantly impair quality of life.

The figures often exist, as they do for air quality and leisure time, but just as these latter figures rarely play into any consideration of national wealth, the former figures rarely come into clinical calculations. Company propaganda has so altered the culture of medicine that it is now difficult to persuade physicians that not treating a mild hypertension is completely different from not treating a fulminant pneumonia. In some cases the figures exist but are withheld by pharmaceutical companies.

A further issue in any contemplation of medical risk management is that these "treatments" commonly act to reverse the effects of lifestyle options. Lipid-lowering drugs may successfully reverse the effects of a diet chronically high in lipids. Antihypertensives may be acting to reverse the effects of a sedentary lifestyle laced with too much alcohol. As Joseph Dumit (2003) has noted, we seem to be moving from a world in which we have regarded ourselves as basically healthy most of the time to a world in which if not actually ill, we are at risk almost all of the time.

Drug treatment's evolution from a medical to a lifestyle framework has parallels with reconstructive surgery's evolution from plastic to cosmetic. Once surgical reconstructive techniques became reliable, they left the domain of specialized plastic surgery and found a wider place in society as commercial cosmetic surgery. The latter is the world in which money is to be made.

Feeding Corporations

In the centre of this story is the clinical trial. Clinical trials evolved to stop fraudulent claims of therapeutic efficacy. The first reactions from ethicists to the notion of randomizing human beings in arrangements for study was that it would be unethical to treat humans as one might treat farm or laboratory animals. But patients volunteered to participate in these trials; at the time many of the drugs were scarce and the agents being researched were drugs such as the antibiotics, which offered potential cures for diseases that posed a risk to both individuals and communities.

Philosophically, the notion that clinical trials prove that treatments work is meaningless in the sense that clinical trials are set up on the basis of a null hypothesis—namely, that a putative treatment in fact does not differ from placebo. If the treatment does appear to differ from the placebo in standard clinical trials, all that can be said is that the treatment does something. This is not the same as saying the treatment works. Far from offering positive evidence, trials offer a quantification of uncertainty.

However, the data that result from such trials have been turned inside out so that trials, which were once designed to stop therapeutic bandwagons in their tracks, have instead become the fuel of therapeutic bandwagons (Healy et al., 2001). Trial data now feed their way into algorithms and protocols drawn up by consensus committees populated by clinicians and other stakeholders with close connections to pharmaceutical companies. The guidelines drawn up by such committees are increasingly seen by health service managers and lawyers as the basis for supposedly rational medicine, and all clinicians come under great pressure to conform their practices to these guidelines.

Furthermore, the data from these trials are the key driver in pharmaceutical company globalization. Globalization hinges on the universalization claimed for scientific methods. The results of these trials are held to apply universally, in Japan as well as America, for children as well as adults, and for all ethnic groups, ages, and sexes. In the 1990s, based on evidence from a selected group of trials that SSRI drugs could not be said to have no effect in the case of nervous disorders, pharmaceutical companies effected an extraordinary change in psychiatric culture, changing cases of Valium into cases of Prozac, Paxil, and Zoloft. In the process, the way we each experience nervous problems was transformed so that we began to see these problems as mood disorders rather than anxiety disorders and began to understand ourselves in terms of fluctuating serotonin levels rather than souls or psyches. None of these changes had a solid basis in science (Healy, 2003a). This story of the transformation of everyday nerves brings home the power of companies to shape cultures—a power that is now being deployed on a global scale.

At the centre of these transformations is the clinical trial and the patients fed into that system. Drugs enter the prescription-only marketplace exclusively on the basis of clinical trials. Clinicians recruit their patients to these trials. The recruitment situation is an ethically fraught one, in which those being recruited are, by definition, vulnerable. In their need and vulnerability, patients want to keep their clinicians happy and in some cases end up participating in trials that clinicians themselves would not participate in. Patients are plunged into risk-laden situations, in which they take risks with agents that pharmaceutical companies, in the process, find are too hazardous to market. They take the risk of suffering drug-induced hazards from drugs that are later marketed by companies that have suppressed the data about those hazards. In addition to taking risks, patients provide their personal details and bodily fluids.

Patients take these risks and allow this invasion of their privacy for free. The voluntary nature of their participation makes pharmaceutical companies the most profitable corporations on the planet. The companies also commandeer the data that results from these trials and assert ownership over it. They select the portions of the dataset that suit their marketing needs and this subset of data is marketed back to us as science, when by definition it cannot be science. At present, however, the entire academic establishment connives in this myth.

Such a scenario might be tolerable if there were good evidence that this process led to improved health outcomes, but there is little evidence to this effect. Within the field of mental health, we now compulsorily detain three times more patients than we did before modern psychotropic drugs were first developed. We also admit fifteen times more patients than before. These patients are more likely to spend time in a service bed now than before modern drugs came on stream, and they are more likely to die from their mental illness now than they were fifty years ago (Healy et al., 2001).

More generally, given that pharmaceutical companies have all but given up on creating drugs that would benefit the community and are focusing instead on blockbusters that have an essentially cosmetic function, it is less than clear that the community should be willing to be fed into the maws of companies that no longer have any community ties.

One method of overcoming the many pitfalls in this situation might be to transform the informed consent in clinical trials into a contract between patients and pharmaceutical companies. Contract law tends to trump other law and might therefore facilitate access to data. The notion of transforming consent forms into contracts comes from developments with Native American communities, who realized that regulatory developments that offer pharmaceutical companies an incentive to do trials in different ethnic groups also offer those groups some leverage in the process.

For many facing the scenarios outlined above, the instinct is to fall back on the assumption that regulators such as the FDA or Health Canada are there in the background protecting them. If these trials have been conducted through the FDA, surely there cannot be anything fundamentally wrong with them. Also common is the belief that the regulators in some way house the raw data; should a problem develop with a drug after marketing forcing the regulatory authorities to consider whether there is a possible causal relationship between the drug and an adverse event, they can consult the data to determine whether the original clinical trials can retrospectively be seen to have offered some cause for concern.

Regulatory bodies, however, function essentially as auditors, rather like Arthur Andersen. It is pharmaceutical companies who decide which trials to conduct. The trials they choose fit the marketing requirements of the company and are not dictated by the nature of the effects of the drug. The trials are conducted in settings and by notional investigators that suit pharmaceutical company interests. Contract research organizations (CROs) are often responsible for the actual running of these trials. In recent years some of these organizations have run trials that included bogus patients. After being discovered, the investigators and others have ended up in jail. These CROs now commonly provide a privatized Institutional Review Board (IRB) system that grants ethical approval to the studies the CRO then runs (Lemmens & Freedman, 2000). The primary criterion for a successful study is the rapid completion of the trial. And the articles that stem from the data collected, tabulated, and analyzed by either the CRO or the pharmaceutical company are written up by medical-writing agencies working for pharmaceutical companies or by the pharmaceutical companies themselves.

One mechanism was put in place to help regulators prevent a pharmacological Enron from happening—these drugs were made available on prescription only. However, while it might have been reasonable to think that physicians had the clout or inclination to grapple with the industry in the 1960s, this is no longer the case. Clinicians are busy celebrating their adherence to the evidence provided by companies.

Coda

The scenario outlined here is one that follows certain rules of the game. One is the availability of drugs on prescription only. A second is the current methods by which drugs are patented. A third is the ability of pharmaceutical companies to claim that data on drugs is proprietary. These rules are not inevitable consequents of the development of psychopharmacological or other pharmaceutical agents. All these rules can be changed.

There are other changes needed. One is to transform public perceptions of risk. We have entered a new culture in which notions of risk are a key currency. For citizens to find their feet in this new culture they need new literacy skills to prevent the perpetration of medical fraud on a gigantic scale.

But finally, quite aside from any change to the rules of the game or any change in the ability of people to disentangle science from quackery, there is the fact that the pharmaceutical companies making essentially cosmetic agents need us far more than we need them. This is a perfect issue for activists and organizers. The research situation provides an almost perfect microcosm of democracy in action—or not in action. What right did I have to present this research? What rights did the subjects in SSRI trials have? Is the silencing of their voices any different from the silencing of those of political prisoners elsewhere in the world?

4
Burying the Messenger
Richard Leitner

When waste management giant Philip Services Corp. set out in May 1992 to woo provincial approval to build a massive industrial dump by the edge of the Niagara Escarpment near Hamilton, Ontario, it might well have been laughed off the face of the Earth.[1]

For starters, the site, a 77-hectare quarry sitting on fractured limestone, was geologically unsuited to containing the toxic leachate the dump would create and required an untested liner system that would have to hold for what the company's own consultants said would be a 300-year contaminating life span. This while the company planned to continue blasting for rock at the site. The quarry was also located near schools, homes, and parks in the fastest growing residential area in Stoney Creek, a suburb on the eastern border of Hamilton. Already home to 13,000 people, the city had an official plan calling for the area to eventually hold 35,000.

Soon Philip would also have history going against it: A virtually identical proposal for a quarry dump near the escarpment in Greensville, a small suburban enclave located on the other side of Hamilton, would be turned down in March 1995 following public hearings before the Environmental Assessment Board (EAB), a provincially appointed independent tribunal.

If that weren't enough, the proposed new dump, officially the Taro East Quarry Landfill, sat next door to an aging, problem-ridden dump, the Taro West Quarry Landfill, also owned by Hamilton-based Philip. As a line of dead trees told anyone who cared to look, toxins from the still-active dump were leaking toward the escarpment, designated a world biosphere reserve by UNESCO in 1990, putting it on par with ecological treasures like the Florida Everglades.

Philip officials liked to claim the old dump was innocuous, but few people knew it was there. Indeed, City of Stoney Creek maps conveniently failed to identify it to prospective homebuyers—the site caught fire in January 1993, the result of a methane gas leak that required the evacuation of neighbouring homes and regular follow-up testing. Adjacent farmers, who still used their wells, reported problems with undersized, sick, and deformed livestock. And because Philip could only contain more widespread contamination from the old dump by sucking up some 500 million litres of leachate and groundwater per year, the company had struck a controversial deal, then characterized as temporary, to send its toxic brew into city sewers despite exceeding bylaw limits for contaminants like chloride and ammonia. Those sewers led to Hamilton's primary sewage treatment plant, also run by Philip as a result of an even more controversial (and ultimately disastrous) ten-year, $187 million untendered contract, regularly cited as one of Canada's privatization horror stories.[2]

Despite these seemingly insurmountable hurdles, the Conservative government of Premier Mike Harris granted Philip the necessary provincial approvals for the new dump in July 1996 without subjecting the project to public hearings—a move that ignored the pleas of key public commenting agencies and area residents and defied a subsequent decision by the Harris cabinet to uphold the assessment board's rejection of the Greensville dump.[3]

It was a victory that trumped the odds, made possible in no small part by the passivity of most local media outlets, in particular the daily *Hamilton Spectator* newspaper. With a newsroom staff of 125, the *Spectator* sets the tone for media coverage in Hamilton; local radio and TV reporters slavishly follow its lead in determining what gets covered and what doesn't. In this instance, the *Spectator* set its tone on coverage of Philip early, offering particularly effusive support for the 1994 untendered contract to operate the region's water and sewage treatment. Although it had never operated a sewage treatment plant, Philip dangled an array of ultimately unfulfilled economic rewards and vowed to make Hamilton an international showcase for water treatment technology. For Hamilton, battered by a killer recession and a declining industrial base, the deal promised jobs, jobs, jobs, and the *Spectator* took on a cheerleading role, welcoming the deal as "a golden opportunity to strengthen Hamilton-Wentworth's reputation as an environmental leader." The sewage contract tied Hamilton's economic fortunes to Philip's corporate fortunes, and more often than not, the *Spectator* and other media players turned a blind eye to a story that was a journalist's feast, one of secret political deals, under-the-table payments, strong-arm legal tactics, and even the use of police powers to intimidate dump opponents.

A rare exception was the paper I worked for, the *Stoney Creek News*, part of Brabant Newspapers, a Southam Inc. chain of weekly papers in the Hamilton area that has since gone through a succession of ownership changes and is now the property of Torstar Corp. Despite having only two reporters, the *Stoney Creek News* staved off legal, political, and economic pressure, giving me free rein to investigate and report on what even the *Spectator* later acknowledged as "one of the most divisive public debates" in the Hamilton area.[4]

In the process, I would be threatened with million-dollar lawsuits, castigated by politicians, informed that our paper had been publicly derided for "advocacy reporting" by the *Spectator*'s senior brass at a public forum, told to watch my back by an anonymous caller, and yanked from the story twice—the second time for good, even though my coverage had by then garnered the *Stoney Creek News* a prestigious Michener Award citation and helped expose a legal loophole, since closed, that allowed Philip to dispose of hazardous cyanide sludge from the United States at the new Taro dump, which was approved only for what the province classified as non-hazardous waste.

The Carrot before the Club
It all began innocently enough. Although our paper had covered the proposed dump sporadically, I decided to write a major feature in June

1994. At the time, a Philip phone survey had indicated four out of five residents in the area were unaware of the plans, a situation that actually made company representatives welcome my interest because they needed to demonstrate a reasonable amount of public consultation to gain approval without public hearings.

Philip's attitude would change as I continued to report on concerns about the project and the company's growing debt, including the $450 million in liens placed against the Taro east and west dumps. The coverage helped spawn Stoney Creek Residents Against Pollution (SCRAP), a citizens group formed to fight the new dump when it became clear it had the tacit, and sometimes overt, approval of politicians at all levels of government.

Philip officials were not happy with developments, as they stressed in a meeting with my publisher, John Young, editor Stephen Beecroft, fellow reporter John Dunford and me in April 1995. Antonio Pingue, a former Ministry of the Environment employee who was now Philip's vice-president of corporate and government affairs, began the meeting with a lengthy rant against our perceived transgressions, often confusing news stories with our paper's opinion-page editorials to accuse us of being biased against his dump project. He also objected to the use of the word "dump," telling us that Philip was proposing an engineered "landfill" that would be far more environmentally friendly than the hole in the ground implied by "dump." Young listened patiently, face reddening, and then calmly defended our coverage and use of the term "dump" to convey, in plain English, the nature of the project. He also explained the difference between editorials and news stories. The lone commitment Young offered Pingue and Taro's general manager, John Fisher, was that we would be as fair as possible in our coverage of an issue of great importance to our readers.

The meeting ended amicably enough, but not before Pingue made an open-ended statement that was subject to interpretation. He asked, to no response, if there was anything his company could do to improve the situation. Philip was already running weekly advertisements in the *Stoney Creek News* pumping the dump proposal, often underneath or opposite our Taro news stories. Our paper, like many Hamilton-area businesses, was still struggling financially from a recession that was only just showing signs of subsiding. It desperately needed advertising revenue, and I left the meeting with the clear impression that Pingue was suggesting we name our price for more favourable coverage. It's a theory we thankfully never tested.

Only afterwards did I learn that this had been the second visit: Company representatives, led by Herman Turkstra, a Hamilton lawyer and former city councillor hired to help navigate the dump approval process, had dropped by earlier, after we ran an editorial cartoon that depicted Bob Hodgson, soon-to-be-deposed mayor of Stoney Creek, blindfolded and poking a big sack of money labelled "Taro East Dump." "Everything looks A-OK to me," read the caption. As a collaborator on the cartoon, drawn by freelancer Gord Boudreault, I knew we had intended to lampoon the mayor's woeful ignorance of the dump project—he couldn't even begin to describe the type of waste it would accept—as he concentrated efforts on a city royalty package. Turkstra apparently felt we were implying bribery. Perspective is everything, as a certain national newspaper likes to say.

Innocuous as they were, the above meetings were a portent of more aggressive actions by Philip as the new Taro dump became a full-blown controversy—at least in the pages of the *Stoney Creek News*—and contributed to Hodgson's defeat in that fall's municipal election. Much of our subsequent coverage would focus on the role of Stoney Creek's nine-member city council, which consistently supported the project, albeit by a 5–4 margin, and conducted many of its deliberations behind closed doors. The secrecy was all the more galling because the city's new mayor, Anne Bain, had trounced Hodgson by promising open government. Among council's more outrageous manoeuvres:

- rezoning the Taro East site for dump uses and placing holding-zone designations on surrounding lands, effectively freezing any potential for development, without required public consultation;

- striking a secret committee in January 1995 to conduct closed-door negotiations on royalties from the new Taro dump, a process that saw city representatives initially seek $72 million—the estimated lost tax assessment from housing that could no longer be built in the area—but settle for $13 million;

- ignoring 133 concerns identified by city consultants hired to review the dump proposal, including the site's location and geological shortcomings, the company's ability to maintain the liner's integrity for 300 years, and potential health, noise, and traffic impacts on the surrounding community;[5]

- striking a secret financial agreement to allow the Taro West dump to exceed approved fill levels when it became clear the site would be full before the new dump was approved—a plan ultimately killed when the Ministry of the Environment ruled the expansion would require an environmental assessment;

- initiating a police investigation to find out how dump opponents learned of the secret west dump expansion plan;

- placing a secret call to a senior ministry bureaucrat, detailed in a memo to a deputy minister, clarifying that council supported the new Taro dump even though a multi-part resolution passed at a massive public meeting earlier that evening was worded to suggest otherwise;[6] and

- opposing an on-site plant to pre-treat the leachate from the old Taro dump before it went into a sewer, an initial condition of Philip's then-temporary deal for the sewer hookup.

Philip's actions were even more disturbing as it sought to prevent dump opponents from derailing a project whose revenues, conservatively estimated at $300 million, were becoming central to its survival. Initially, the company wooed the community with royalties, promises of a new corporate head office (never delivered), and small but highly publicized donations, including $100,000 to the Hamilton Region Conservation Authority to plant trees at a popular beachfront park on

Lake Ontario—a donation pulled after the public agency called for hearings on the new dump. Philip even attempted to "balance" the views of opponents by arriving at one conservation authority meeting with a new group of pro-dump Stoney Creek "residents" in tow. The group lasted until the next issue of our paper, the period it took to expose, with one phone call, that its spokesperson, Chad Ferrara, was Philip's manager of business development and other members were employees.

But the company soon took on a far more threatening tone, one taken seriously because of rampant rumours that it had ties to organized crime. While publicly protesting what he characterized as ethnic smears, Philip president Allen Fracassi didn't help perceptions by appearing at public meetings to huff and puff and badger those who dared to oppose his new dump. When Stoney Creek council succumbed to public pressure and finally held a special meeting on the project at an elementary school near the site, a fleet of big Philip rigs circled the block while burly drivers stood at the entrance doors. Two police officers were on hand—a first in my experience, but repeated at a subsequent public meeting—and escorted SCRAP's leader, Brad Clark, to his car in the dark afterward. People who placed lawn signs opposing the dump reported threatening phone calls. After I appeared on the CBC's *Fifth Estate* program for a story on the dump controversy, I received a call from a man who wouldn't identify himself but told me Philip was the type of company to use whatever means necessary to get what it wanted. "You've got a lot of balls to say those things about those guys on national TV," he said, in what I took as either a warning or a veiled threat.

Although Allen Fracassi consorted with a known gangster, no one has ever offered any evidence to substantiate Philip's rumoured Mafia connections.[7] But the reputation struck fear in some dump opponents. A troubling case in point is Victor Veri, an eccentric local watchdog and unsuccessful candidate for council. Veri had challenged the city's decision to rezone the Taro east quarry and surrounding lands without the required public process. In a highly unusual move, the Ontario Municipal Board agreed to hear Veri's appeal even though he'd missed the appeal deadline, and the public anxiously awaited the showdown. But just days before the hearings were set to start, Veri withdrew his appeal, claiming he couldn't afford the fight. In what it claimed as a show of good faith, Philip announced it would help pay Veri's legal bills. Citing a confidentiality agreement, Veri declined to comment and all but disappeared from public view. When questioned about the deal by the CBC's *Fifth Estate*, Philip lawyer Herman Turkstra maintained, on air, that all was above board, rejecting suggestions Veri had been paid off.[8]

Turkstra, to put it charitably, was wrong: Acting on a tip, I managed to wring the details of the deal out of Veri by claiming I had enough information to go with a story with or without his help. It was a complete bluff, but Veri obviously wanted to clear his conscience. He confessed he had in fact received $35,000 to cover his expenses, ones he had told others were in the $12,000 range. He had also received a second "consulting" contract with a Philip subsidiary worth $50,000—for which he had yet to do anything. Although we gave the story big play, I went easy on Veri: He insisted he'd been motivated less by money than concern for his continued well-being.

One might expect under-the-table payments to alarm politicians, but Stoney Creek Mayor Anne Bain reflected the general laissez-faire attitude of government officials toward Philip. "That happens with big companies all the time, right?" she said, declining to judge Philip's or Veri's actions when I called her. "If I'm not involved in it, I'm not going to comment."

When All Else Fails, a Legal Sledgehammer Will Do

But Philip's biggest weapon against its critics was legal action, often taken in measures so disproportionate to perceived transgressions as to draw attention to the company—and its growing financial problems. The most spectacular example is its response to an October 1995 letter written by a former employee to then Ontario Environment Minister Brenda Elliott during the formal public commenting period on the new Taro dump. Michael Hilson, a Hamilton resident who had worked in Philip's accounting department, levelled some eye-popping charges against his ex-employer in a five-page letter outlining reasons why he felt the company couldn't be trusted to operate the new dump. Among his allegations:

- Philip had failed to account for an estimated $30-million disposal liability for "well in excess of 100,000 tonnes" of hazardous electric arc furnace dust, a steel-making by-product it had been stockpiling at an abandoned Firestone tire factory in Hamilton;

- Philip president Allen Fracassi had deliberately misled company directors to believe a money-losing cleanup venture, estimated to be $10 million in the red, was in fact profitable, a claim likely to curry favour on the Taro project with the Ministry of the Environment, which otherwise would have had to foot the cleanup bill; and

- Philip kept its employees in line through deceit, higher-than-standard pay, intimidation and harassment, and firing those who dared to disagree with senior management.

Hilson called senior Philip executives "among the most unethical people (business or otherwise) that I have ever come to know," concluding they were likely to illegally dispose of the stockpiled hazardous waste at the new Taro dump. When a source provided me with a copy of the letter, part of the formal public record, I didn't know what to do with it because the contents were so blatantly defamatory. So I did what most reporters do: I consulted others, providing a copy via facsimile machine to a stockbroker who had helped me understand the intricacies of big company finances as well as to a second source. Philip showed no such hesitation, reacting in what would become a characteristic manner: it filed a $30 million suit against Hilson, characterizing him as a disgruntled employee who had a drinking problem and was seeking to exact revenge for his dismissal from its acquisitions branch the previous year. The company also insisted the allegations were false and, without any apparent sense of irony, in breach of Hilson's fiduciary duty of confidentiality. If being sued for $30 million didn't intimidate Hilson, surely the method of serving notice did: a private investigator handed him the package as he was preparing to perform master of ceremony duties at a cousin's wedding in Las Vegas. The big figure and libel chill likely also explains why no media opposed Philip's successful bid to obtain a draconian judicial order (since lifted) sealing the letter and court file and preventing Hilson or anyone from discussing or publishing anything to do with it.

Soon after, I received a subpoena to appear for an examination for discovery for the lawsuit. I allegedly was among Hilson's "co-conspirators" who, although only referred to as "John Doe, Jane Doe and Other Persons Unknown," were also being sued for $30 million. Philip claimed we were deliberately trying to drive down the value of its shares for personal gain by selling short—that is, selling loaned shares at a high price on speculation that their price would fall by the time we had to pay for them. There were two problems with this scenario. First, although Philip's stocks had declined by $1.30 at the time—to about $10—they soon rebounded and there was no evidence that Hilson's letter played any role in their fall or rise. More important from my perspective is that I hadn't even heard of Hilson at the time of his letter and had never owned any Philip shares or even played the stock market.

I don't remember much from my examination for discovery encounter with Philip lawyer Herman Turkstra other than that I declined to swear on the Bible and left angry at our lawyer for providing no help whatsoever in maintaining our initial goal not to divulge to whom I'd provided copies of the letter. She gave Turkstra a warm greeting at the outset—they obviously knew each other—and mostly sat in silence as he peppered me with questions and ran down a list of people, asking if I'd ever been in contact with them. By deduction he identified the stockbroker, but not the other source. I left feeling like I'd dodged a bullet, as I'm sure did many of the ten others hauled into a downtown Hamilton office for the same grilling. They included Mark Morrow, then Stoney Creek's New Democratic Party Member of Provincial Parliament (MPP), several dump opponents, local cable TV-show host Terry Ott, *Hamilton Spectator* reporter Kate Barlow, and, curiously enough, Hamilton police detective David Broom. Broom refused to answer Turkstra's questions, which focused on an apparently ongoing police investigation into Philip.

Disciplining Dissent

Terry Ott, the quirky host of *It's Your Call*, a cable phone-in TV show that spiritedly ridiculed Philip and local politicians, claimed the company and Mayor Anne Bain played a key role in the abrupt cancellation of his program shortly thereafter. Certainly, neither had any love for Ott, who had a knack for nicknames. Bain, for instance, became "Anne Shame," although Herman Turkstra became "Count Turkstra"—a reference to Count Dracula that mocked the lanky Philip lawyer's profession and wild-eyed glare when staring down opponents. I became Woodstein—a contraction of Woodward and Bernstein, the *Washington Post* reporters famous for bringing down Nixon—an epithet that lampooned our paper's meagre resources but, according to Ott, was meant as a personal compliment. Perhaps Ott's most memorable moment came when Bain and I appeared on his show just after she had defeated Bob Hodgson. I nearly fell off my chair when Ott followed a brief introduction with his first question to Bain: "So, what's changed, other than the skirt?"

To the Woodshed and Back

Although Ott's ouster attracted little interest beyond the pages of the *Stoney Creek News*, Philip's reaction to the Hilson letter found a wider audience, attracting the attention of Paul Palango, an investigative reporter and author who would work as a freelancer on the first of two stories on the dump controversy by the CBC's *Fifth Estate* program. My paranoia was such that when Palango dropped by the *Stoney Creek News* offices to talk to me in December 1995, I didn't trust him: I thought he might have been hired by Philip to trick me into saying something slanderous that could be used in litigation. Palango tried to convince me of his credentials by giving me a copy of an exposé he'd written for a local business magazine on the controversial firing of the general manager of the Hamilton Tiger-Cats football club. I remained suspicious. My mind was put at ease, though, when he dropped by with a larger contingent from the CBC to discuss the dump saga. One of Palango's co-researchers was Harvey Cashore, a school chum from my days at Carleton University who would go on to co-author *The Last Amigo*, a best-seller that investigated alleged government kickbacks during Prime Minister Brian Mulroney's reign. I remember feeling

Burying the Messenger

both energized and relieved: the big boys were in town to tell the country about the funny business surrounding the dump's push toward approval; it was my time to shine.

The relief would be short-lived. I can still recall vividly the morning of February 19, 1996, when I reached Taro's general manager, John Fisher, asking him to comment for a story I was working on for that week's paper.

"Hasn't your publisher spoken to you?" he asked.

"No. Why?" I replied.

Fisher said the company had sent a letter to publisher John Young on Friday. It was now 10:30 A.M. on Monday and I was working to a noon deadline. "I think you better speak to your publisher," he said, and we ended the conversation.

I confronted my editor, Stephen Beecroft, who knew nothing of the letter. He went into the publisher's office, returning to inform me that John Young was pulling all of my Taro-related stories and an editorial I had written criticizing city council's belated decision to hold an open house to solicit public input on the dump compensation plan it planned to pass the following Monday. Outraged, I went to see Young myself. He told me to close the door as I entered his office and pulled a thick folder from a drawer in his desk as I sat down. Young confirmed that he had received a letter from Philip and told me he was yanking our Taro coverage because the company was threatening to sue us for millions of dollars if I wrote another word about Philip or the dump project. The letter sat on top of a stack of other letters he'd received from Philip, all apparently raising concerns about our coverage and my role in particular.

I was dumbfounded, especially since Young and I often discussed the dump and our coverage of it. Young told me that in addition to the letters, he had also been getting regular calls from John Fisher demanding to know who wrote the unsigned editorials on our opinion page—something Young had, as is customary, refused to divulge since editorials are the opinion of the paper, not the author. I asked to see the latest letter. Young initially refused to hand it over, relenting only on the stipulation that I couldn't have a copy—a violation of our union contract far from my mind at this point. Written by Philip lawyer Herman

Turkstra, the letter essentially alleged I was an environmentalist with "a hidden agenda" against Philip and the Taro dumps. Turkstra cited as evidence my decision to pass on copies of the Hilson letter to two sources, again claiming I was part of a conspiracy to drive down Philip stock prices. He also drew a bizarre connection to a story written by another reporter for another of our chain's papers on Philip's attempt to win the contract to run Hamilton's airport, a bid that failed largely because of growing criticisms of the company's local influence, which included the aforementioned untendered contract to operate Hamilton's sewage system. The airport story, according to Turkstra, demonstrated that our papers were also part of a conspiracy against Philip and its owners.

I laughed. "You can't be taking this seriously?" Young agreed the conspiracy theory was preposterous. He also told me that at no time had Philip pointed out inaccuracies in my reporting, which made what followed all the more hard to swallow: I would no longer be allowed to cover or write about issues related to Philip and Taro. "We, as a company, are not sure that you don't have a hidden agenda," Young said. He told me it was widely known within Brabant Newspapers that I was "somewhat of an environmentalist." I couldn't believe my ears, especially since, again, I had regularly discussed the story with Young and received nothing but encouragement until that point. I was now being sent to the gulag for thought crimes. I can't remember much of what was said after that, but I recall feeling as though my soul had been sucked out of me as I limped back to what I jokingly called my horse stall—a makeshift cubicle Beecroft had crafted from economy two-by-fours and cheap rec-room panelling. An apologetic Beecroft told me he would go to the open house on the compensation package and John Dunford, our other reporter, would cover a meeting organized by SCRAP for the next evening.

Not ready to go down without a fight, I sat down and pounded out an angry letter to Young, copying it to our chain's president, Paul Winkler, as well as Southam Inc. president Gordon Fisher. I took particular umbrage at the charges that I was an environmentalist with a hidden agenda, pointing out that as an old-school journalist, I had made a point of not joining any political or environmental organizations. I did admit to being concerned about the environment in my community and beyond: "Call it freedom of thought, opinion and belief, values I thought we, as newspapers, would uphold and defend," I wrote. I concluded by again outlining the circumstances in which I had shared Hilson's letter, which at the time had been part of the public record, available to anyone who made the trip to the Ministry of the Environment's headquarters in Toronto. With the CBC still working on its story, I wrote that our response to Philip would come under wide scrutiny and affect our credibility for years to come. "Ultimately, if reporters aren't able to discuss and share information with sources who have an understanding of matters beyond reporters' expertise, reporters cannot do their job. Reporters are not experts, which is why we call those who have the apparent expertise. If we cannot make preliminary inquiries about matters which are potentially defamatory without worrying about landing in court, freedom of the press under The Charter is meaningless."

Within the week, I was back on the story. As I would learn from Dunford and the CBC crew, my removal from the story was a hot topic at a well-attended SCRAP meeting. I had become a temporary *cause célèbre* and Young's phone rang all week. Paul Winkler, our chain's president, also intervened. As the leader of our workplace's union, I hadn't endeared myself to Winkler, but we'd shared an enthusiasm for the Taro story, which he saw as an example of the ability of community newspapers to deliver in-depth coverage of local issues. We struck an agreement: I would continue to cover Taro but cease writing editorials for our opinion page. "You have a lot of friends," Young told me afterward. To his credit, he was magnanimous about the entire episode. And, despite the agreement with Winkler, Beecroft let me continue writing editorials—a situation made easier because Young and Winkler left the company shortly thereafter.

The Taro controversy continued to rage in the ensuing months, but nothing fazed local politicians or the Harris government, which approved the dump that July: not the national exposure from the *Fifth Estate* highlighting the tortured approval process and Philip's ham-fisted legal tactics; not yet another lawsuit, this time against journalist Paul Palango for $11 million over a provocative speech he gave to the Women's Canadian Club of Hamilton,[9] a suit announced in a press release given to a *Spectator* reporter before Palango even gave his talk; and certainly not a succession of *Stoney Creek News* stories on ongoing affronts to due process, including the Victor Veri payoffs and the secret machinations of local politicians in apparent violation of Ontario's Municipal Act.[10] Although several formal commenting agencies opposed the dump, only the Hamilton Region Conservation Authority, responsible for safeguarding the local watershed, called for public hearings—a move that would lead Hamilton councillors to later dump its long-time chair, Al Stacey, who had tipped a tied vote in favour of the hearing request. The Niagara Escarpment Commission, although opposing Taro as "virtually identical" to the rejected Greensville dump, opted against calling for hearings, saying funding cuts under the Harris government left it without the resources to participate.

The dump's approval didn't end the fight between citizens and those who had rammed the project down their throats. Or the funny business. At the request of a neighbouring farmer, a Ministry of the Environment enforcement officer dropped by the old Taro dump unannounced at the end of that July, taking groundwater samples at the site and adjacent farms. According to those on hand, Philip went ballistic and the samples sat untested in a fridge until the ministry's district manager, John Percy, ordered them dumped down the drain, an episode typical of the local ministry office. (It was, for instance, Victor Veri who pointed out to the ministry that the old Taro dump had exceeded approved fill levels, a revelation that played a key role in that site's closure.) But the real fight took place on a community liaison committee Philip was required to form as part of its certificate of approval for the new dump. Opponents filled the citizen positions and the committee soon became the forum for disputes over every aspect of the dump. They ranged from neighbours' ongoing complaints about odour and dust to Philip's resistance to pay for an on-site ministry inspector as stipulated in its certificate and the company's controversial bid to also send leachate from the new Taro dump into city sewers.

A Brief Moment in the Sun

The *Stoney Creek News* meanwhile found itself briefly in the national spotlight, nominated in April 1997 for the Michener Award for public service journalism. I was sky-high when I found out and bounded off to the office of our new publisher, Cal Bosveld, to break the good news. His reaction might have raised red flags at the time, but I took it as evidence of his being a bit of a skinflint. Bosveld had come to our chain as part of a deal that saw Southam buy his family's small family paper in the Hamilton suburb of Flamborough. Even though we stood in stellar company with the *Toronto Star,* CBC, *Le Devoir,* and *St. John Times Globe,* he treated the honour as if it were some run-of-the-mill industry award. He told me to drive up by car and find a reasonably priced hotel for the necessary overnight stay but initially refused to let editor Stephen Beecroft go. The Michener Award is no small deal; invitations are hand-delivered by a Queen's representative, and the award ceremony and dinner is hosted by Canada's governor general—Romeo LeBlanc at the time—at Rideau Hall. Beecroft, who emigrated from Britain and held the monarchy in high esteem, told me he planned to attend regardless. Although Bosveld's attitude put a damper on the moment, he eventually relented and agreed to pay for our flights to Ottawa and hotel accommodations and even offered to take pictures at the event, for which he had also received a hand-delivered invitation. But at the anointed hour, Bosveld was a no-show and hadn't sent regrets, even though he had told me he was planning to be in Ottawa that weekend for a family gathering. An embarrassed Beecroft filled in when organizers asked for our publisher to join other nominees' executives in an anteroom. I sat in a rented suit in the peanut gallery with his wife, Ginny, who was giddy with excitement over the pomp and ceremony. We didn't win—the *Toronto Star* took the award for a heart-wrenching exposé of the failings of the judicial system on spousal assault cases—but were treated to an obscenely lavish dinner accompanied by plenty of mutual back-slapping as nominee representatives explained the circumstances of their stories. Beecroft told me afterward that while in the anteroom with the other bigwigs, he'd been forced to correct, somewhat sheepishly, *Toronto Star* publisher John Honderich when he crowed that no Southam paper had been nominated—a slap against new owner Conrad Black, an arch-conservative and big fan of the monarchy who reviled the *Star* for its liberal slant.

Other accolades followed, but the Michener nomination gave Beecroft and me our fifteen minutes of fame: We were featured in *Maclean's* magazine under the headline "Small but dogged" (in which Philip characterized me as "a hopelessly biased environmentalist bent on destroying the project")[11] and included in a cheesy photo spread on "The Faces of Courage" in a glossy Hamilton magazine.[12] Brad Clark, the leader of SCRAP, would meanwhile challenge Mayor Anne Bain in that fall's election, running under the slogan "The People's Voice, The People's Choice." A political neophyte, he shocked veteran observers by coming within 29 votes of unseating Bain in a five-way race that also included Bob Hodgson, the mayor she had succeeded, and Mark Morrow, now the former NDP MPP. Bain, who had spent twice as much as Clark on her campaign to capture only slightly more than 30 percent of the vote, was stoic: "I'm proud of everything I did. I wouldn't change a thing," she said, blaming the *Stoney Creek News* for the tight race.

Cyanide Sludge Hits the Fan

Although that might have been the final chapter on the Taro saga, it was a story that wouldn't go away, even had we wanted it to, because Philip's financial house of cards began to collapse, just as Michael Hilson had predicted in his October 1995 letter. The slide into bankruptcy began in November 1997, just after Bain's re-election, when the company issued a prospectus as part of a 20-million-share offering on the Toronto and New York stock markets. Philip's shares, which had been trading in the $10 range at the time of the skirmish over the Hilson letter, had reached an all-time high of $27.91, and the company's net earnings had been steadily increasing despite its massive debt—at least according to the prospectus.[13]

On January 26, 1998, though, Philip dropped the first of many bombshells, announcing that it was restating its earnings for 1995 through 1997 to reflect mounting losses as a result of US$125 million in missing copper inventory, which it blamed on "rogue" trading by one of its executives, Robert Waxman, whose family's business had been a prominent player in the Hamilton scrap industry before being gobbled up by Philip. Philip and Waxman began suing each other. The fallout saw Philip share prices plummet and the flow of red ink soon became a tidal wave. Shareholders on both sides of the border launched class-action suits over allegations the company had known about the copper losses and other financial problems prior to issuing its rosy prospectus. By the time Philip held its annual meeting in June 1998, it was staggering under a $US1.1 billion debt and share prices had dropped to $2.18 on the Toronto Stock Exchange. At the meeting, company executives announced that a number of Philip properties would be put up for sale—including the new Taro dump.

Locally, there were plenty of other developments to keep Philip and Taro in the news, including the company's bid to send leachate from the new Taro dump into Hamilton's sewer system; controversial proposals for a golf course and sports park by the old dump; and plans for more housing by both sites. This as Philip's own annual report on the new dump, required as part of its operating approvals, revealed what many had suspected: leachate from the old dump had begun to migrate southward, away from the escarpment, toward homes along Mud Street, a main arterial road—and Philip had known about it for five years.[14] Why wasn't anyone raising hell? A trip to the local land registry offered a possible answer: the company had been quietly buying homes along Mud Street and had used a numbered Ontario company to pay a local developer $2.4 million for a seven-hectare vacant property zoned for residential development. Developer Losani Homes had purchased the land for $1.15 million in 1993, turning a tidy profit four years later without even having to put a shovel in the ground.

Fred Losani, the company's vice-president, didn't return my call for the September 9, 1998, front-page story, but I soon heard from him after it ran. He was furious. He told me people were insinuating he'd taken hush money from Philip—perhaps because he'd quietly disappeared after publicly raising concerns about the new Taro dump's impact on neighbouring development plans prior to its approval. But then Losani pointed out an error in my story, an admitted rookie mistake for someone not conversant with land registry documents: I'd missed a payment that had reduced Losani's profit to $900,000, not the $1.25 million suggested in my story. Still pretty easy money, in my view. I quickly agreed to correct the record, but Losani was not mollified, vowing to call my publisher. Losani and Cal Bosveld were both directors of the Hamilton-area real estate board, but I didn't give it much thought at the time, even when Bosveld dropped by to discuss the story with me—the first time he had ever done so on any story. I explained the circumstances, noted we had corrected the record the following week, and took Bosveld at his word that he planned to smooth things over with Losani. I would learn much later that Bosveld in fact began talking to editors about moving me out of Stoney Creek to a split-beat position at our two smallest sister papers on the other side of Hamilton.

If indeed that had been the plan, it may explain his hollow reaction to a huge development concerning the new dump, one that made it nearly impossible to move me. At the *News*, we had already been poking around the Hamilton processing plants Philip used to treat waste before shipping it to Taro. With the help of Brad Clark, the leader of the anti-dump citizens group SCRAP, we had found an insider who agreed to take pictures of the infamous hazardous electric arc furnace dust detailed in Michael Hilson's letter and grab a sample of waste stored at the same plant. The insider's tales were troubling, but tests of the waste sample failed to produce a smoking gun. That would change dramatically thanks to some top-notch legwork by Michael Hilson and journalist Paul Palango, who had been using a Yahoo! on-line chat room on Philip to investigate the company's ever-deepening financial crisis and ongoing allegations about its waste-management practices.

In September 1998, the pair drove down to the Detroit headquarters of Michigan's Environmental Protection Agency (EPA) to study records of Philip's shipments from two of its subsidiaries there. (Unlike in Ontario, where you have to file a request under freedom of information legislation and hope you might see at least some documents within six months, United States EPA offices furnish records for photocopying on request.) Hilson and Palango were shocked by what they discovered: since the new Taro dump began operating in December 1996, Philip had imported at least 634 truckloads of hazardous waste into Hamilton from the two Detroit plants—more than twelve times the number in the year leading up to the site's opening. Nearly three-quarters of those shipments came from a company known as Cyanokem Inc., a generator of three categories of cyanide wastes. The balance, from subsidiary Petro Chem, were petroleum wastes. In the United States, those wastes could only go to a hazardous waste dump; they could not be mixed with other wastes or "treated" to render them suitable for a site like Taro, which was only approved for so-called non-hazardous wastes.

Palango and Hilson returned to Hamilton with copies of the documents and made some initial inquiries at the Ministry of the Environment's Hamilton office. They then contacted Toni Skarica, Tory MPP for the suburban Hamilton riding that had successfully fought the similar dump project in Greensville. Skarica had been among the few local politicians to speak out against the Taro dump and Philip's corporate tactics. He arranged an evening meeting with Palango that would include myself, *Maclean's* magazine reporter John Nicol, in town to do a story on Philip's troubled finances, and Brad Clark. Palango provided copies of the documents and we agreed to work collaboratively to get to the bottom of the story.

What followed was easily my most exciting experience as a journalist. I began my inquiries that week with a call on Tuesday to Carl Slater, a supervisor in the ministry's local office who had always been decent and forthright with me. Slater said his office had been unaware of the Detroit shipments but he understood the cyanide-laced sludge from Cyanokem was being properly processed by Philip before going to the Taro dump—although he couldn't divulge that process, as it was "proprietary." Although he didn't know where the petroleum wastes were going, Slater told me, "We know for a fact it doesn't go to Taro"—an assertion he would soon retract. Philip, which by now insisted that all my inquiries be submitted in writing, also insisted it was treating the waste properly. "Taro does not accept hazardous waste," it stated in a written response the following day. Both sides were essentially singing from the same songbook. The tune changed, though, after I called George Rocoski, a senior bureaucrat in the ministry's Toronto office. Rocoski told me Ontario also had no-mixing laws on certain hazardous wastes. I read out the US hazardous waste classifications on Philip's shipping manifests from Detroit and asked if they were also considered untreatable hazardous waste in Ontario. Dead silence. After a long pause, Rocoski simply said he would look into the matter further and get back to me. He never did. But late Friday afternoon, I did get a phone call from a ministry spokesperson that would require me to rewrite my story for that week's paper. It would be a happy task: Philip had been ordered to stop sending the Detroit wastes to Taro and the ministry was launching a formal investigation into the matter. I was ecstatic and rushed over to Bosveld's office: "Got 'em!" I beamed, punching the air. He had been made aware of the Detroit shipments but seemed strangely subdued given the implications of what became a national story.

We played the story big: "Taro clipped on cyanides" screamed our front-page headline above a photo of a Philip truck entering the Hamilton processing plant that had accepted the Cyanokem wastes—mixing them with cement, a treatment it dubbed "Ecosafe." I hastily wrote a hard-hitting editorial under the rather cheeky headline "Cyanara, Philip." Any hopes of a total scoop were dashed that evening, when Brad Clark appeared in a story on the ministry's investigation on CTV's national broadcast. The *Hamilton Spectator,* caught flat-footed, as on most big Philip and Taro developments, ran a brief front-page story the following day based almost entirely on the CTV broadcast. Clark and others familiar with the story refused to talk to *Spec* reporters before we went to press—payback for years of perceived mistreatment—forcing the daily to go with an odd follow-up story that typically, if in this case unintentionally, predominantly presented the company's side under the tell-tale headline "Cyanide charge rejected: Philip says Taro clean."[15]

Maclean's meanwhile opted against reporting the cyanide controversy as part of a bigger Philip story, leaving the *Stoney Creek News* to reveal the full details five days after the CTV broadcast (a fact that reportedly led the *Spectator*'s then editor-in-chief, Kirk LaPointe, to throw our paper across the newsroom in anger).

Community furor over the Michigan shipments was the most intense I've witnessed in my sixteen years as a journalist. The first of several public meetings deteriorated into an unruly shouting match, fuelled by a mother's periodic screams at ministry and Philip officials as the meeting's chairperson did his best to maintain decorum. Everyone was under suspicion: politician, bureaucrat, even citizen members on the community liaison committee struck to oversee the dump. A humbled Stoney Creek council asked the province to close the dump. Ontario's environment minister, Norm Sterling, promised a full inquiry, to include all of Philip's processing plants in Hamilton.

I meanwhile continued probing all aspects of the story, including Philip's quiet efforts to gain approval to "process" for disposal at Taro those hazardous electric arc furnace stockpiles recounted in Michael Hilson's October 1995 letter. The ministry took a beating over two revelations: that an inspector had given Philip advance warning its Cyanokem shipments would be tested and that the daughter of the top boss at the ministry's Hamilton office had been given a summer job at a Philip subsidiary. I would tag along with the *Fifth Estate*'s Harvey Cashore, in town to do another story on Philip, on a trip down to Detroit to visit the Cyanokem plant, a rundown operation in a poor, predominantly black neighbourhood, and to examine records at the Michigan EPA office. Those records showed the Philip plant had federal approval to ship fourteen solid and liquid hazardous wastes to Hamilton and was part of a trend that had seen Canada's imports of hazardous waste more than triple since the advent of free trade—a development expert observers attributed to weaker environmental laws governing their disposal.[16]

Karl Marx's aphorism that history repeats itself, the first time as tragedy, the second time as farce, seemed to rule the coming months. Philip served notice of its intention to sue the CBC over the *Fifth Estate* story, which had essentially relayed much of what had already been published elsewhere, including in the *Stoney Creek News*. But the threat struck many as comical this time around because the company didn't appear to have the money for such fights. Foretelling its eventual bankruptcy, its stocks were now trading in the 30¢ range following an announced $US1.1 billion loss in the first nine months of 1998. Philip could no longer make payments on its $US1.645 billion debt and was even in arrears on an insurance policy for the Taro dump.

Brad Clark, the leader of SCRAP, meanwhile decided to run for the government that had approved the Taro dump, replacing the incumbent MPP Ed Doyle as the Tory candidate in the upcoming June 1999 provincial election. A former TV reporter, Doyle had been elected in

Disciplining Dissent

1995 as part of the so-called Common Sense Revolution espoused by leader Mike Harris. Although the Tories remained popular provincially, Doyle had a big problem. During the 1995 election campaign, he had vowed to press for public hearings on the new Taro dump. "Dump the dump," he told high school students when queried on his position. Once in office, Doyle had a selective memory: he told me he remembered his "dump the dump" remark, but not his vow to fight for public meetings—made while holding a megaphone at a SCRAP rally organized by Clark. Landing Clark was a big coup for the Tories, effectively curing their local Achilles heel.

One Enemy Too Many and It's Off to the Hinterlands
A bigger development for me personally was that I now had a new "senior editor," Mark Cripps. Stephen Beecroft had suffered a variety of ailments over the preceding years, and the company had established the senior editor's position to perform his desktop publishing duties. Cripps, who came to us from the *Prescott* (Ontario) *Journal*, brought a new ethos to the *Stoney Creek News*. Upon his arrival, he trashed the Ontario Liberal Party and its leader, Dalton McGuinty, in back-to-back editorials—shredding our paper's traditional non-partisanship. Cripps made it clear from the outset that he was a big fan of Mike Harris's Common Sense Revolution, a prescription of tax and spending cuts, asserting it was impossible for Ontario to have a recession under Tory rule. He boasted about enjoying warm relations with Bob Runciman, a right-wing Tory cabinet minister whose riding included Prescott, while speaking disdainfully about unions in general and ours in particular. Cripps told me he enjoyed writing economic development stories and planned to diversify the paper's coverage and lessen our focus on Taro and Philip issues.

Beyond some feisty political discussions, I didn't get to know him much during his initial weeks on the job because we were in the throes of labour negotiations. As the union chair, I was often booked off for bargaining sessions that were the nastiest in my experience. Over the years, many publishers had introduced themselves by telling me unions have no place in a community newspaper environment; it seemed written into their job descriptions. Yet Cal Bosveld was a different breed. Where other publishers either bent, or were broken, on the way to a middle ground, he was inflexible. He also bargained from a position of strength. Southam's owner, Conrad Black, vilified unions, and Mike Harris had just weakened Ontario's labour laws. Add in Bosveld's own apparent antipathy toward unions and you had a recipe for the most hostile negotiations in ten years. Bosveld and our union negotiator, Peter Murdoch, nearly came to blows at one point.

After going through the whole collective bargaining dance—conciliation, mediation, and strike deadline—we reached a tentative settlement for a contract that offered annual 2 percent wage increases over three years, fairly standard at the time. I was so incensed by the company's hard line on some issues that I was prepared to strike, but few others were itching for a fight with Conrad Black (wisely, in retrospect, given disastrous experiences at the *Calgary Herald* and *St. Catharines Standard*). Adding to my fury was the company's insistence that it would only pay a $375 signing bonus to our one hundred or so members if the bargaining committee presented its "final offer" without comment. All five committee members opposed the deal, but both we and the company knew we'd be hung out to dry if we kissed off the bonus to make what may have been a petulant political point. So we swallowed and agreed to muzzle ourselves. After the vote, which ratified the new contract by a two-thirds margin, I broke my silence, ripping the company for what I saw as an insulting attitude toward the value of its employees, those on the lower end of wage scales in particular. Two weeks later, I was informed my days at the *Stoney Creek News* were over.

It was shortly after noon on Monday, May 31, 1999, a deadline day, that Bosveld's brother Ken, whom he'd hired a year earlier as managing editor, called me into his office—the second week in a row he had done so. The week before, he had raised concerns about my productivity for the previous two issues. I admitted my performance hadn't been up to usual standards—we had been in the heat of bargaining—and asked to take a week's vacation in June to recharge my energies. I thought Ken might have still been smarting from my angry outburst over changes he'd made to an editorial I'd written on tax cuts, a major issue in the provincial election then underway. Cripps and I had apparently agreed on the content—essentially, that tax cuts came with a price—but the final version had gone through a first-ever editing by Ken to include the assertion that "Tax cuts are certainly an effective tool in improving Ontario's tax competitiveness, which helps create jobs. This is a priority." I objected strenuously to what I viewed as a near-direct lift from the Tories' re-election campaign slogan, "Tax cuts create jobs."

When Ken called me into his office for that first meeting, he didn't mention the editorial and his tone was pleasant enough, so I didn't dwell on it. I'd never had any previous complaints about my job performance, and since bargaining was now over, I was ready to get on with reporting. But at the second meeting, Ken told me he was about to issue a company memo announcing my transfer to a split-beat position at our two smallest papers, the *Dundas Star* and *Ancaster News*—an assignment so unpopular the previous two reporters had quit. Ken asked what start date to put on the memo, given my request for a week's holidays. When I objected to the move, he made it clear it was not up for debate, claiming I was required to beef up news coverage at the smaller papers in anticipation of the launch of a competitor paper by Torstar (no such paper ever materialized). I told him I'd take my week's vacation and only go to my new assignment under protest.

This time, there would be no reprieve. Brad Clark, who would win the riding and later become a minister in "mentor" Mike Harris's cabinet, had complained to Cripps a week earlier, after I'd pressed the premier to tell Stoney Creek residents what he planned to do about the dump his government had approved without public hearings. In town for a circus-like campaign pit stop that featured a "spend-o-meter" lampooning the alleged tax-and-spend proclivities of the opposition Liberals, Harris ignored my presence and inquiries as he glad-handed his way out the door and into a waiting van, two body guards wedging me aside. When I protested to Clark, he insisted an election campaign was no time to discuss such complexities because Taro was still under investigation. His complaint to Cripps didn't stop Clark from including a photo someone had taken as I grilled him after Harris's visit in a full-page election advertisement in the *Stoney Creek News*. The inference that I supported Clark's election bid turned my stomach.

Although several readers called to protest my transfer, there would be no angry public meeting. One vocal dump opponent was given a weekly column to massage his concerns. Anne Varangu, the first resident to raise concerns about Taro, wasn't so easily rebuffed, drafting up small posters that she stapled to telephone poles in town. As I headed out of town for my new position, I can still recall the surreal feeling as I drove along Stoney Creek's main street, yellow "Reinstate Richard Leitner" posters bidding me goodbye as I passed each telephone pole.

At the time, I thought my transfer had more to do with my union role than my reporting, and not without reason: Within six months, the company would fire two members of our bargaining committee, at least one, in my view, on severely trumped up charges. We also had a protracted legal fight over the company's failure, in our view, to properly post job openings in the editorial department, effectively barring me from applying for any new positions—including at the *Stoney Creek News*.[17]

Although our side consistently took the position that my transfer was motivated by anti-union animus, others have told me my reporting prompted the move. As the story goes, Mayor Anne Bain and local business leaders met with my bosses and threatened to hurt the *Stoney Creek News* economically if our news focus didn't change. In their view, the Taro controversy and ongoing publicity over the hazardous waste shipments were bad for business, especially for developers wishing to build houses in the area. Certainly, the Stoney Creek Chamber of Commerce, of which Bain had been president before becoming mayor, had always supported Philip—even if its membership didn't play along. Prior to the dump's approval, the chamber's new president, Dennis McKay, a big Bain booster, had invited Taro general manager John Fisher to address a monthly breakfast gathering. A red-faced McKay cut Fisher's presentation short after a handful of hostile questions. "The one thing that puzzles me is, why would you put something like that in the middle of the city?" demanded one small business owner, reflecting the room's mood. "You're going to put in a liner, so there must be something that you're afraid could happen." The ongoing negative publicity surrounding Taro undoubtedly grated on Bain and local builders: cyanide sludge doesn't sell homes or elect politicians.

This story has one final bizarre twist. A lengthy investigation into the Detroit shipments by the Ministry of the Environment's enforcement branch concluded with a report severely criticizing Philip's waste processing operations and the local ministry office's slipshod oversight.[18] Yet contrary to initial assertions by local ministry staff, lead investigator Gord Robertson concluded Philip hadn't broken any laws by mixing registered hazardous wastes for disposal at Taro because of a technicality: Although the province had published an industry-accepted manual on the no-mixing rule, the manual hadn't been promulgated as law. An embarrassed Harris government quickly closed the legal loophole by cabinet decree in September 1999. At a press conference announcing the move, out-of-town reporters goaded Tony Clement, the province's new environment minister, into apologizing to the citizens of Stoney Creek. Philip meanwhile sued the ministry for $20 million for wrongly alleging that it had broken the law. Since then, little has changed on the Taro front despite Clement's appointment of an "expert panel" to review the site's operations. There is still no health study (recommended by the panel), no actual sampling to see what wastes were present in the dump at the time the cyanide sludge hit the fan, and the dump's leachate now goes into city sewers despite also exceeding bylaw limits. As I write, Philip (now a new corporation based in Houston, Texas) is in a legal battle to change Taro's operating licence to disband the community liaison committee that oversees the dump.

It's said all that's needed for evil to flourish is for good people to do nothing. No one can say the *Stoney Creek News* did nothing. It went beyond the call of duty, more often than not with the support of bosses. Politicians must answer for their own actions, but that they stood by Philip through thick and thin is not altogether surprising. Hamilton is an economically depressed city that has seen job-producing industry in steady decline. Philip was to be the new player in town and successfully sold itself, initially at least, as a company that would be on the leading edge of environmentally responsible waste management. That two rough-and-tumble local guys, Allen and Philip Fracassi, were at the helm only added to the allure of cheering for the home team, especially as the company became, however briefly, top dog in North America.

It is the Fourth Estate's role to hold politicians and institutions like corporations accountable. In this respect, blame for the Taro debacle must rest squarely on the shoulders of Hamilton's media. Although the *Stoney Creek News* wielded little influence beyond its readership, the same is not so for the *Hamilton Spectator*. And on Taro and Philip issues, the *Spectator* either took the company's side or usually looked the other way.

An example of the former is a "special report" the *Spectator* ran on the dump as it steamrolled toward approval. Apparently embarrassed into action by the CBC's arrival in town for the first of two *Fifth Estate* documentaries, the paper assigned a star reporter, Andrew Dreschel, to the report. He spent six weeks researching for a two-part series that, atypically for the *Spec* back then, began on the front page. The first installment's headline set the tone: "War of Words."[19] Absent of any discussion of the actual merits of the dump, Dreschel's story instead highlighted a dozen quotes to reinforce his underlying theme that the Taro fight could be boiled down to a mere war of words. "Puffed by half-truths and innuendo, the landfill fight has taken on a life of its own that has even seasoned politicians marvelling at its intensity," he told readers without itemizing those "half-truths" or probing the reasons behind the intense feud. Although Dreschel touched on some of the racier developments, like the Hilson letter imbroglio and Victor Veri's secret payoff, he did so only in sparing detail as he moved to his main theme that it was all a "war of words."

Anyone hoping for more in the second installment was quickly disappointed. A front-page story, under the heading "Talking Tough: Philip Environmental Meets Gossip Head On," gave Philip CEO Allen Fracassi an exclusive forum to attack the "oft-repeated speculation that the hometown company that's enjoyed spectacular growth has organized crime connections."[20] "This underworld connection—what kind of BS is that?" Fracassi asked, playing the race card to explain criticisms of Philip amid its phenomenal growth. "Somehow they turn that around to be, 'Hmmm, I don't know, he's Italian and he grew up in the North End, so hey, 90 per cent chance this guy has got underworld money.'" Dreschel acknowledged it was unclear who "they" were, but left little doubt how he personally felt about Philip: It had "a reputation for innovation" and wasn't "going to let a local landfill controversy stand in the way of its global ambitions."

In case readers still harboured doubts about the company, Dreschel tackled Philip's image problems in a full-page feature inside titled, "Uncharted Waters: Philip Pays a Price for Going Where Others Would Not."[21] Attributing those problems to a "hungry, super-aggressive" competitive ethos that showed no hesitation "to lobby politicians for contracts or go over the heads of local regulators," according to Dreschel the company's desire to continually be "going forward" led it to occasionally step over the line—as during a dispute with the Ministry of the Environment over Philip's unauthorized disposal of hazardous electric arc furnace (EAF) dust at its non-hazardous dump in Sarnia. Dreschel dismissed the incident as the exuberance of "a hard-driving company that can't take no for an answer," an attitude that "may sometimes take them [*sic*] into uncharted waters." To support this view, he paraphrased a local Ministry of the Environment official's apparent assertion that the dispute was more of an administrative, rather than an environmental, concern.

The real story is in fact striking in its parallels with the dispute over cyanide wastes at Taro. In this instance, Philip had, by its own account, dumped 9,400 tonnes of "processed" hazardous EAF dust at its Sarnia dump over a nine-month period before a tip drew the ministry's attention.[22] As with the cyanide sludge, EAF dust was considered a "listed" hazardous waste, meaning it always remained hazardous, even when mixed with cement. And contrary to Dreschel's assertions, there was considerable disagreement between the ministry and the company over the legality and environmental safety of Philip's practice of mixing EAF dust with cement to bind its heavy metals—the so-called "Ecosafe" treatment. Philip claimed its processing created a new waste that fell within non-hazardous limits. But a senior ministry engineer took quite another view, arguing the cement had "a masking effect" on the standard toxicity test. "The long-term leachability [of cement-mixed wastes] is unknown from this test," he contended.[23]

After a prolonged dispute, Philip ultimately received approval to dump up to 110,000 tonnes of the waste in Sarnia—over that community's objections—in return for agreeing to far more stringent limits on the cement-mixed waste's concentrations of hazardous metals than in the 9,400 tonnes it had already dumped there. One wonders how the real story might have affected the debate over the Taro dump, which had already accepted the cyanide sludge by the time I obtained the Sarnia documents.

A poignant example of the *Spectator* looking the other way occurred during a discussion of Philip's controversial sewer hookup for the old Taro west quarry dump's leachate at a March 1996 meeting of Hamilton's regional environmental services committee. As part of its initial deal to hook into the sewer, Philip had signed a written agreement to construct an on-site pre-treatment plant by July 1995, estimated to cost $8.6 million to build and $1.7 million per year to run. But eight months after the deadline, Philip wanted to explore alternatives, including amending the city's sewer-use bylaw to make the Taro leachate legal. Hamilton councillor Geraldine Copps—mother of Hamilton's renowned federal Liberal Member of Parliament, Sheila—was livid. As she set off a heated discussion, Shaun Herron, a *Spectator* reporter who was sitting to my right at a table provided for local media, snapped down his pen and steno pad on the table and leaned back, folding his arms across his chest. Until then, Herron had been taking notes on other agenda items and his actions were so deliberate, I did a double take before returning to scribbling furiously on my own steno pad, also taping the debate as I usually did to ensure accuracy. Obviously, no story ran in the *Spectator*. Herron has since been promoted into the paper's management ranks.

In the interest of full disclosure, let me confess that, in a pique, I applied for a job at the *Spectator* after my own employers transferred me out of Stoney Creek, reasoning that if I was to be relegated to the backwaters I might as well be better paid for it. When I called to inquire if there were any openings, the paper's deputy editor, Dana Robbins, enthusiastically invited me to drop by for an interview. I knew Robbins as a union colleague from the days before he shifted into management ranks, so I had a good feeling about his warm response to my call. I realized I'd misread the situation shortly after the interview began.[24] I provided copies of my work, including some of my more investigative stories on Taro and coverage of a controversial proposal for an expressway through Hamilton's Red Hill Valley that the *Spectator* supported. Robbins told me his boss, editor-in-chief Kirk LaPointe, was a big fan of "contrarian thinking." He asked me if I had written or read any stories falling into that category. I told him I felt my sample stories fell into that category because they went against prevailing business, media, and political climate in favour of the dump and expressway. But I had missed the concept, according to Robbins: Most people expect opposition to dumps, for instance, and believe they are bad for the environment. "Contrarian thinking," he told me, "would be that a dump is good for the environment." Our conversation went from bad to worse and I left without asking when I could expect to hear back from him. Robbins has since become the *Spectator*'s editor-in-chief.

Although the *Spectator* alone must answer for its non-coverage—perhaps it, too, bought into the Philip dream—editors there evidently didn't hold the *Stoney Creek News*'s approach to the Taro/Philip story in high regard, accusing us of "advocacy reporting" when criticized for their own coverage. The charge is not without foundation: our paper did advocate for public hearings on the dump and, with help from like-minded individuals, assumed the role of community watchdog once the site opened because the institutions normally charged to fulfill that task failed the people of Stoney Creek miserably. Yet the accusation also assumes that silence is not also a form of advocacy. By its inaction, the *Spectator* effectively sided with Philip and politicians against the community. It helped to stifle dissent. Had the *Spectator* been more critical, it's possible Philip might indeed have been laughed off the face of the earth when it proposed to put its dump in the middle of a growing community near the edge of the Niagara Escarpment. Instead, it was given licence to write one of the most sordid chapters in Hamilton's history.

5

Industry and Academic Biotechnology: Teaching Students the Art of Doublespeak

E. Ann Clark

Academics generally take pride in making effective, articulate, well-reasoned arguments. Skill in both written and oral expression reflects an in-depth understanding of the nuances of the language of choice. Increasingly, however, language is being misused by some academics, intentionally and overtly, to achieve goals at variance with those of academia.

I speak of the encroachment into academia of a genre of discourse I will call "doublespeak," a term I explain below. Evidence of the widespread adoption of doublespeak as standard policy by industry and government will provide a foundation for more detailed coverage of its adoption by some professors, and more alarmingly, by students under their guidance. I focus specifically on the students because their involvement illustrates the progressive, pervasive infiltration of the values of the proponents of doublespeak into Canadian universities. The values borne by these doublespeak apprentices will influence not simply the future professoriate, but the place of academia in society.

What is "Doublespeak"?

The term "doublespeak," as used in this paper, draws inspiration from the terms "Newspeak" and "Doublethink" coined in George Orwell's chillingly prescient novel *1984*.

Newspeak is intended to replace conventional English (Oldspeak) by allowing only words that pertain to proper thoughts. Screening the dictionary regularly to eliminate undesirable words—words that might have unorthodox meanings—is expected to control thought itself:

> Don't you see that the whole aim of Newspeak is to narrow the range of thought? ... Has it ever occurred to you, Winston, that by the year 2050, at the very latest, not a single human being will be alive who could understand such a conversation as we are having now? ... The whole climate of thought will be different. In fact, there will be no thought, as we understand it now. Orthodoxy means not thinking—not needing to think. Orthodoxy is unconsciousness. (Orwell, 1949)

Doublethink is an ideology of acceptance of intentional and perpetual fabrication. Everything is subject to continual revision and reinterpretation by the Ministry of Truth, inculcating the citizenry to acknowledge contradiction as a normal part of life:

> Winston sank his arms to his sides and slowly refilled his lungs with air. His mind slid away into the labyrinthine world of doublethink. To know and not to know, to be conscious of complete truthfulness while telling carefully constructed lies, to hold simultaneously two opinions which cancelled out, knowing them to be contradictory and believing in both of them, to use logic against logic ... to forget whatever it was necessary to forget, then to draw it back into memory again at the moment when it was needed, and then promptly to forget it again: and above all, to apply the same process to the process itself. That was the ultimate subtlety: consciously to induce unconsciousness, and then, once again, to become unconscious of the act of hypnosis you had just performed. Even to understand the word "doublethink" involved the use of doublethink. (Orwell, 1949)

Doublespeak. The new term combines Newspeak and Doublethink as 'Doublespeak': expression intended to deceive, to mislead, and to control, using not simply words but orchestrated strategies of contradiction. An example of doublespeak has been provided by a tenured assistant professor at a Canadian university, who stated, "In the midst of all of this confusion over GE [genetically engineered] foods, there has been an abandonment of educational leadership.... Lamentably, these people are not doing what they are paid to do: to think critically and provide well-informed decisions.... Scientists abdicate their leadership responsibilities and leave students to form their opinions in a sea of websites, conversations rooted in caffeine-stimulated intuition, and conspiracy-theory speculations."

Why this statement should be considered doublespeak will be clarified at the end of this paper.

Industrial Applications of Doublespeak

Some industries have found it prudent to manipulate the public, including government, to safeguard profit-making opportunities. This is particularly true for corporations engaging in business practices that might not withstand public scrutiny. To control public access to information, it has become standard practice for such corporations to employ firms specializing in what is euphemistically called "public relations" (PR)—or more bluntly, doublespeak. For example, Monsanto hired two PR people to attend the trial of Percy Schmeiser, a Saskatchewan canola grower being sued by Monsanto for patent infringement (see below, under "Student Doublespeak"). Their job included speaking to the press during court breaks, to provide Monsanto's version of the proceedings, and distributing press releases summarizing the salient points of the favourable testimony of Monsanto's chief witnesses as soon as they finished testifying but before they were cross-examined.

The Father of PR

Much of the art of contemporary doublespeak traces back to Edward Bernays, who was the son of Sigmund Freud's sister and, reportedly, a man of enormous ego and incessant self-promotion. Among his many lasting contributions was a book published in 1928, unabashedly entitled *Propaganda*. A quote gives both the flavour of the man and the foundational assumption of the contemporary doublespeak industry:

> The conscious and intelligent manipulation of the organized habits and opinions of the masses is an important element in democratic society. Those who manipulate this unseen mechanism of society constitute an invisible government which is the true ruling power of our country. (Cited in Rampton & Stauber, 2001)

Applications of his thinking, both by himself and by more contemporary players, are shown in the following examples (adapted from Rampton & Stauber, 2001):

Edward Bernays, on behalf of American Tobacco Co., sought to get women to smoke by using cigarettes as symbolic of the women's liberation movement. He encouraged debutantes to march in the 1929 New York Easter Sunday parade while smoking cigarettes—for which he coined the term "torches of liberty" in order to convert socially unacceptable behaviour into something admirable to women of the era: defiant independence.

Edelman Public Relations Worldwide, on behalf of Microsoft, opposed anti-trust investigations in eleven states by giving the appearance of public support for Microsoft. The firm planted articles, letters to the editor, and opinion pieces in newspapers as "spontaneous" testimonials to create "leverageable tools" for the company's lobbyists in the form of a dossier of positive press clippings. The strategy was exposed when an anonymous whistleblower released a large binder of confidential documents to the *Los Angeles Times*.

The same firm, in the same case, tried to lend professional credibility by placing full-page ads, "Open Letter to President Clinton from 240 Economists," from the Independent Institute—surreptitiously funded by Microsoft —to obscure the issues and deflect blame to others. This time, the strategy was exposed when a second set of documents was leaked to the *New York Times* (actually generated through dumpster diving by a rival PR firm).

Industry and Academic Biotechnology

The Timberlands Debacle

PR firms employ a range of doublespeak methods, as detailed in a text by Denise Deegan (2001). A representative repertoire is seen in the work of the PR firm Shandwick New Zealand on behalf of its client Timberlands West Coast Ltd. (Hager & Burton, 1999). Timberlands is owned by the New Zealand government and is responsible for logging New Zealand forests. Environmental groups sought to protect remaining old-growth native forest lands on the west coast of the South Island of New Zealand. Documents leaked by an insider afford unusually frank insights into an eight-year counter-campaign orchestrated by Shandwick, at the behest of Timberlands, whose tactics can be summarized as follows:

- attempt to discredit and marginalize opponents publicly, using specific value-laden words such as "eco-terrorist," "misinformation," and "extremist";

- send "moles" to attend conservation group meetings to source information/discredit them;

- photograph and videotape participants in anti-logging protests, and track, monitor, and respond to every letter to the editor, public comment, or innuendo—always "have the last word";

- threaten protesters with legal action (analogous to SLAPPs [Strategic Lawsuits Against Public Participation] used in the US);

- seek to identify financial weaknesses in critics and undermine sources of funding;

- screen journalists writing unfavourable articles and apply pressure/complain to editors and provide lavish opportunities for site visits to sympathetic journalists and politicians;

- write school principals whose students were involved in a protest, threatening legal action;

- pressure an environmentalist academic/complain to vice-chancellor of her university, then provide modest funding to other academics and employ them for credibility (see "Third-Party Technique," below);

- create a front group that appears to represent community interests and fund a range of community activities, especially sporting events, to generate public support;

- ghost-write letters to the editor to be signed by local residents;

- exaggerate statistics on logging and employment;

- physically destroy a treetop protest site by helicopter to intimidate protesters;

- repeatedly remove protester graffiti each time it reappears; and

- divide and conquer environmental groups/misrepresent importance of those sympathetic to the cause. (Adapted from Hager & Burton, 1999)

Third-Party Technique
This method deserves special emphasis because it has become so popular with some academics. Rampton and Stauber (2001) describe the "third-party technique" in the words of Merrill Rose, executive vice-president of the Porter/Novelli PR organization: "to put your words in someone else's mouth."

The advantages of the third-party technique are many:

- it offers camouflage, hides vested interests, and lends credibility;

- it encourages conformity to a vested interest while pretending to encourage independence; and

Industry and Academic Biotechnology

- it replaces factual discourse with emotion-laden symbolism.

An employee of Burson Marsteller, the largest PR firm in the world, put it this way:

> For the media and the public, the corporation will be one of the least credible sources of information on its own product [and] environmental and safety risks.... Developing third party support and validation for the basic risk messages of the corporation is essential. This support should ideally come from ... political leaders, union officials, *relevant academics,* fire and police officials, environmentalists, regulators. (Little, 1990, emphasis added)

Public Backlash
However, the behind-the-scenes efforts of PR firms have become increasingly transparent, leading to negative public perceptions. In 1999, the Public Relations Society of America (PRSA) and the Rockefeller Foundation released results of a survey employing a National Credibility Index to "measure trust in a person advocating or espousing a position" (quoted in Rampton & Stauber, 2001). PR professionals came forty-third out of forty-five, after "famous athletes" and just before "famous entertainers" and "TV or radio talk show hosts."

It does not seem implausible that similar disrepute will follow those, including academics, who employ the same philosophy. That is, of course, if they are exposed as such. The essence of PR—both within and without academia—is secrecy. As explained by Rampton and Stauber (2001), "the best PR ends up looking like news.... You never know when a PR agency is being effective; you'll just find your views slowly shifting."

Government Applications of Doublespeak

Richard Nixon's "dirty tricks" campaign is arguably the best known, but certainly not the best run, doublespeak campaign. Government application of doublespeak is known by various names, including "public affairs" and "spin doctoring." Donovan et al. (1981) stated forthrightly, "in the real-life political arena, none of the participants ... will behave in an intellectually honest fashion.... [Instead, they] will distort the advantages of their positions and the disadvantages of their opponent's. They will shade the truth—first for their audiences; then in many cases, for themselves." Although doubtless always true, and not just in politics, doublespeak has attained new prominence with the tightening of industry-government linkages.

One example of government doublespeak in Canada relates to the unqualified promotion of GM (genetic modification) in agriculture. Freeze (2002) cited evidence obtained by Brad Duplisea through Access to Information protocols that Agriculture and Agri-Food Canada (AAFC) and the Canadian Food Inspection Agency (CFIA) jointly allocated $3.3 million over five years to promote the perceived safety of GM foods to Canadians, including $2 million for direct mailings to households, with at least $1 million in other communications. Articles reportedly ghost-written by the CFIA were inserted into *Canadian Living* and *Coup de Pouce* starting in July 2000, at a cost of $302,000 (Abley, 2000). At least $700,000 was funnelled through the Food Biotechnology Communications Network (FBCN) located in Guelph—an organization that purported to offer objective information to interested consumers. Other "third-party" recipients of government funding to promote biotechnology were the Consumers' Association of Canada and the National Institute of Nutrition (Freeze, 2002).

To cite a specific example of doublespeak, consider the wording of *Biotechnology in Agriculture,* a glossy colour pamphlet jointly produced by the CFIA and AAFC, in CFIA0012:1997:

- *Biotechnology in Canada:* The opening question, "What is Biotechnology?" is answered by "Do you eat bread, cheese, or use antibiotics? Then you have been enjoying the fruits of biotechnology."

  Doublespeak Principle: Framing the question in this way narrows the range of thought and encourages buy-in to the technology by trivializing the very real differences between conventional breeding and genetic modification.

Industry and Academic Biotechnology

- *Biotechnology in Canada:* The section on "How Will Biotechnology Affect You?" claims "biotechnology will have major payoffs for Canada's economy.... It is creating opportunities for farmers, food processors and distributors to sell new or improved goods in Canada ... enabling farmers to achieve greater yields."

  Doublespeak Principle: The phrases "creating opportunities" and "new and improved goods" offer attractive symbolism. In reality, roughly 99 percent of GM hectarage is sown to either *herbicide tolerant* crops (for instance, Roundup Ready canola) that promote dependence on proprietary herbicides or *insecticidal* crops (Bt) of uncertain environmental impact. The benefit to consumers is virtually nil.

- *Biotechnology in Canada:* "Biotechnology Working for You" implies that disease-, pest-, and stress-tolerant crops; nutritionally enhanced foods; healthier animals; chemical substitutes; and disease diagnostic kits are the products of biotechnology.

  Doublespeak Principle: Extolling the hypothetical, and as yet unrealized, virtues of presumptive GM crops is more attractive symbolism. With quite modest exceptions, these claims have not come to fruition in the intervening five years.

Nowhere in the document, or for that matter in any more recent government document, is there a hint of the significant, unanswered questions that have been raised in the refereed literature (reviewed by Clark & Lehman, 2001) by the Royal Society of Canada's Panel on the Future of Food Biotechnology[1] or through on-farm experience. Coverage is so one-sided that you'd assume government documents were actually written by Monsanto if you missed the small logo in the corner of the front cover.

The Canadian government fails to acknowledge—anywhere—that it has made no attempt to document the purported advantages of GM crops for anyone apart from the proprietors. A hand-picked group of individuals was appointed by the Canadian government to serve as the Canadian Biotechnology Advisory Committee (CBAC), with the mandate "to optimize the economic, health, safety and environmental benefits of biotechnology." To assist in its deliberations, the CBAC commissioned thirty-five separate reports.[2] Of the thirty-five, at least fourteen deal with patents and protecting intellectual property rights. In the only report that assesses the costs and benefits of GM crops, Harley Furtan, chair of Agricultural Economics at Saskatchewan, wrote: "As of January 2001 there is no publicly available survey or data on how individual farmers have benefitted from the adoption of GM crops in Canada. Therefore, it is not possible to say how much economic benefit farmers have experienced from adopting this technology" (Furtan & Holtzman, 2001).

Is it at all plausible that the Canadian government would abstain from surveying farmers and publicizing the results if the crops actually did what had been promised—produced higher yields, reduced pesticide application, protected the environment, improved farmer profit, or fed the world's hungry? As a result of this curious disinclination, government is left with a vacuum of substantive evidence to justify annual expenditures of hundreds of millions of taxpayer dollars to support the GM industry. Instead, it's reverted to increasingly desperate and transparent efforts at doublespeak—with the same effect on public opinion as that experienced by industry.

Public Backlash

As occurred with industrial applications, use of doublespeak has reduced the credibility of government "in the public good." Government has failed miserably in its efforts to manage public outrage at being involuntarily obliged to consume GM foodstuffs. Bill Leiss (2002), who holds the Natural Sciences and Engineering Research Council/Social Sciences and Humanities Research Council (NSERC/SSHRC) Industry Research Chair in Risk Communication and Public Policy at the University of Calgary, was forthright in his assessment. He admonished the Canadian government against continued involvement in GM promotion if it wishes to regain credibility as an independent promoter of the public good.

Academic Applications of Doublespeak

Orwell (1949) said, "those who control language, control the debate." With apologies to Orwell, I would expand his reference to "language" to *communication,* and in the present context to *education*—namely, "those who control education, control the debate." Those entrusted with graduate education frame the research questions and methods that solidify the values of the students they supervise. And what some are doing today under the umbrella of academic freedom is actually not far removed from the proclamations of Orwell's Ministry of Truth.

The chilling effect of industrial encroachment on academic freedom is increasingly viewed as a threat to academia as we know it. The withdrawal of public good" funding and the requirement for matching funds to access what is left effectively control the research questions that we can ask, and hence, the lessons our students can learn, as seen by the following dialogue in the October 2002 issue of *University Affairs* (Toomey, 2002):

> *Brian Ellis, Associate Director, University of British Columbia Biotechnology Laboratory, and co-chair of the Royal Society of Canada's Panel on the Future of Food Biotechnology*: "It's my conclusion, having watched the biotechnology scene over the past 15 years, that the universities have been remarkably quiet about these issues of regulation and the consequences of biotechnology.... [We] don't see any concerted efforts within the university community to begin addressing the related questions ... from health to impacts on our economic system, particularly in agriculture, but also in the health-care sector."

> *Alan Wildeman, Vice President Research, and Director, Food System Biotechnology Centre at the University of Guelph*: "The role of the universities is to pursue knowledge so that policies ... are ... based on fact rather than on conjecture, speculation, purely economic motives, or fear mongering.... All of that is going on right now."

Unreported in the article were Dr. Wildeman's views on what—if anything—any Canadian university, including the centre he directs at

Guelph, is doing to address the substantive regulatory issues of the downstream health and environmental impacts of agricultural biotechnology.

Few cases are as obvious—or as contentious—as the November 1998 purchase (lease?) of an entire department at the University of California, Berkeley—the Department of Plant and Microbial Biology—by Novartis (now Syngenta). In a five-year deal, Novartis paid $25 million for first rights to negotiate licences to patents on specific discoveries made by the department as well as for two of the five seats on the committee charged with selecting research projects (Buchanan & Chapela, 2002). It was disheartening to observe a number of graduate students at the International Workshop on the Ecological Impacts of Transgenic Crops at Berkeley in March 2000, energetically papering the audience at our evening on-campus seminar with thick information packets bearing the Novartis logo. It is difficult to image a professor, let alone a graduate student, in this department even contemplating research into anything other than the potential benefits of GM products.

Industry interest in publicly funded institutions as venues for research may be fading. The £50 million, three-year-old alliance between Syngenta, the John Innes Centre, and the Sainsbury Laboratory is being dissolved at the instigation of Syngenta.[3] The John Innes Centre is an independent research centre supporting over 850 staff and students. The threat that industry funding will channel university research away from societal needs and compromise the integrity of the university as a source of unbiased information may subside if industry finds it more expedient to restrict its funding to in-house research.

However, the long-term legacy of industry encroachment may well be more insidious as a result of professors who have chosen to become "the third party," as referenced above. Of many contemporary examples, C. S. Prakash of Tuskegee University, who operates the influential AgBioWorld Web site established in conjunction with Greg Conko of the Competitive Enterprise Institute, is perhaps the best known.

The impact of such professors is prolonged and indeed exacer-

Industry and Academic Biotechnology

bated when they enact their third-party role—replacing factual discourse with value-laden diatribes to camouflage and further the goals of external vested interests—through the very graduate students they are entrusted to teach. These are the students who will replace us and inculcate in the next generation the values and skills of doublespeak.

Based on his experience as a professor at Berkeley (see above), Ignacio Chapela (personal communication, 2002) offered unique insights into the rationale for teaching doublespeak to graduate students. He noted that targeting sophomoric students with a thirst for seeing their names in print has multiple advantages:

- avoiding the exposure of advisors (both in the faculty as well as in the PR campaign);

- lightening up the style with rhetorical and stylistic daredevil jumps that more mature writers would not dare take;

- providing easily "burnable" figures in case their statements turn out to be too damaging; and

- establishing a new generation of fire-tested and technically conversant proselytes for "the cause."

He concluded by adding that this is a "great testament to the maturing of the PR [I think it is appropriate to call it propaganda] campaign."

Student Doublespeak

Evidence that students are already mastering the art of doublespeak is not hard to find. Just one of many examples is an article posted September 6, 2002, to a Canadian university Web site regarding the case of Percy Schmeiser, a seventy-one-year-old Saskatchewan canola grower being sued by Monsanto. The article had a link to the Monsanto Web site[4] and later appeared in the *National Post*. A graduate student had written it, emulating the distinctive writing style of the faculty adviser who was quoted at the start of this paper. A critical analysis of the student's article reveals his efforts to use intentionally misleading wording, innuendo, and ridicule—the standard tools of doublespeak—to discredit and diminish without actually addressing the substantive issues raised by the Schmeiser case.[5]

Four selected quotes from the student's article are presented below, followed by the apparent inference or intent, the substantive evidence to refute the intended message, and finally, a short comment on the doublespeak principle being invoked for each quote.

- *Student Text 1:* "Big-bad multinational Monsanto dragged Schmeiser into court after it was suspected that he had been growing a GE Roundup Ready variety of canola and had not been paying the licensing fees that thousands of other Canadian farmers had willingly paid. A Canadian federal court ruled in 2001 that he had indeed infringed Monsanto's patent."

    Inference: That Schmeiser intentionally grew and benefited from something he'd not paid for.

    Rebuttal: "The uncontradicted evidence of Mr. Schmeiser was that he has never purchased Roundup Ready Canola and has never signed a TUA[6] relating to Roundup Ready Canola. Monsanto had initially alleged that Mr. Schmeiser had somehow acquired Roundup Ready Canola in 1997 but that allegation was withdrawn along with all claims of infringement with respect to Mr. Schmeiser's 1997 canola crop." (Para. 18, Court of Appeal)

    Third-Party Doublespeak replaces factual discourse with emotion-laden symbolism: "Big-bad multinational," "dragged into court," and "other … farmers had willingly paid" are symbolic innuendos intended to leave impressions at variance with the facts of the case as expressed by the Appeals Court judges themselves.

    Comment: Inferring that Schmeiser should have been paying licensing fees obscures the fact that the gene had encroached involuntarily on his farm—and was in fact a nuisance rather than a benefit to him. Also ignored is the issue of patent rights over property rights, industry's inability to contain proprietary genes, and the implications of same for farmers and society as a whole.

- *Student Text 2:* "Schmeiser has stood by his defence that the GE canola was blown into his field by passing seed trucks and then cross pollinated his crop, resulting in the detectable traits; at least until a few months ago, when Schmeiser took a new tack, declaring that he had indeed deliberately planted the Roundup Ready canola, but that as a farmer, it was his right to brown bag seed or purchase it from a neighbour."

Inference: That Schmeiser intentionally planted brown-bagged seed (for instance, bought fraudulently from an unscrupulous neighbour instead of from a seed dealer) and hence, denied Monsanto its technology fee.

Rebuttal: "Only the Schmeiser canola crop for 1998 was found to infringe the Monsanto patent. That crop came mainly from seed saved from the glyphosate resistant canola found on and adjacent to the Schmeiser property in 1997. However, the Trial Judge did not reach any conclusion as to how glyphosate resistant canola came to be there in 1997, because in his view it did not matter." (Para. 47, Court of Appeal)

Third-Party Doublespeak uses deliberate fabrication to encourage conformity to a vested interest: As a lifelong seed saver, Schmeiser is a tireless advocate for the right of seed saving and for seed sharing among neighbours as traditionally practised in most farm communities around the world even today. He has never said that he obtained patented seed fraudulently or encouraged others to do the same.

Comment: Endless repetition of allegations of brown bagging—allegations that directly contradict the publicly accessible findings of the Courts—is reminiscent of Orwell's doublethink. Either the student had access to information that was somehow missed by the investigative power of Monsanto or the intent is deliberate misinformation.

- *Student Text 3:* "Stompin' Tom Connors sang a song that if it weren't for copyright laws (not that Schmeiser has shown much respect for legally-protected things) would probably become Mr. Schmeiser's theme. A line of the lyrics reads: I'm a poor, poor farmer, what am I going to do? Now that he has been instructed to pay Monsanto's court fees of $153,000, he really will be."

Inferences: That Schmeiser has not shown respect for the law; that Schmeiser is getting what he deserves for breaking the law.

Rebuttal: Schmeiser is a law-abiding citizen with a long record of public service. He served as town councillor for the Town of Bruno from 1960 to 1963, and mayor from 1964 until 1983. He was a Member of the Legislative Assembly (MLA) for the constituency of Watrous in Saskatchewan from 1967 to 1971. He was appointed to and served on the Saskatchewan Real Estate Commission from 1990 to 1999. He has no criminal record.

Third-Party Doublespeak replaces factual discourse with emotion-laden symbolism: Publicly disparaging an opponent, particularly under false pretenses, is stock-in-trade doublespeak. As shown by the documented activities of Shandwick on behalf of Timberlands (Hager & Burton, 1999), practitioners of doublespeak feel no obligation to remain within the facts of the case.

Third-Party Doublespeak hides vested interests: Does undisguised gloating over the misfortune of others serve the interests of academia and society—the intent of academic freedom? Or, considering the Monsanto link to this paper, does it serve external interests whose goals may be contrary to societal needs?

- *Student Text 4:* "Schmeiser has been preaching a tale of corporate omnipotence, but only after getting caught with his hand in the cookie jar. His rants against corporate rule have nothing to do with the safety of genetically engineered foods. It appears that good old Percy, practical as are most farmers, wanted to use a product that worked but didn't want to pay for the technology."

Inferences: That Schmeiser intentionally used the RR gene for personal benefit (hand caught in the cookie jar); that Schmeiser's primary argument relates to food safety.

Rebuttal: "His 1998 canola crop was mostly glyphosate resistant, and it came from seed that Mr. Schmeiser had saved from his own fields and the adjacent road allowances in 1997. Although the Trial Judge did not find that Mr. Schmeiser played any part initially in causing those glyphosate resistant canola plants to grow in 1997, the Trial Judge found as a fact, on the basis of ample evidence, that Mr. Schmeiser knew or should have known that those plants were glyphosate resistant when he saved their seeds in 1997 and planted those seeds the following year. It was the cultivation, harvest and sale of the 1998 crop in those circumstances that made Mr. Schmeiser vulnerable to Monsanto's infringement claim." (Para. 58, Court of Appeal)

"The uncontradicted evidence of Mr. Schmeiser is that he did not spray Roundup on his 1998 canola crop. The Trial Judge did not say whether he believed Mr. Schmeiser on that point or not, because he concluded that spraying with Roundup was not an essential element of the alleged infringement." (Para. 29, Court of Appeal)

Third-Party Doublespeak uses deliberate fabrication to encourage conformity to a vested interest while replacing factual discourse with emotion-laden symbolism: To benefit financially, Schmeiser would have to have sprayed the herbicide Roundup (glyphosate) to realize the only benefit offered by the patented Roundup Ready gene—namely, simplified weed control. Monsanto did not contest his sworn statement that he did not spray Roundup. Thus, far from having his hand in the cookie jar, Schmeiser was simply the unwitting recipient of uncontainable gene flow.

Comment: The oblique reference to food safety—an issue that has never been central to Schmeiser's case—is an effort to deflect attention from the substantive issues that *are* central to Schmeiser's case. It may also be an attempt to rationalize why this article should be posted at a site ostensibly focused on "food safety."

In the same article, the student acknowledges having read the Appeals Court decision: "The appeal panel unanimously rejected all of Mr. Schmeiser's 17 points of contention, leaving only the Supreme Court of Canada as the last refuge for legal appeals." Thus, the contentions in the posted article cannot be excused due to ignorance and can only be interpreted through the lens of doublespeak.

Public Backlash
As has already been demonstrated with examples from industry and government, professors who embrace the principles of doublespeak are eventually exposed, to their discredit and that of their employer. In an article entitled "Rude Science,"[7] editor John Morriss (2001) reviewed the performance of a tenured assistant professor (whom we shall call A. P.) at a Canadian university.

John Morriss stated:

> ... at some point, [A. P.] morphed into a full-blown apologist for biotechnology, while still operating under his "food safety" umbrella.... More serious are [A. P.]'s aggressive if not vicious attacks on other scientists who dare to challenge his views. The *National Post* piece—as part of "Junk Science Week" was a particularly offensive attack on no less than the Royal Society of Canada and the members of the panel it appointed to review food biotechnology.... [A. P] dismissed the report as "a document that more resembled a Greenpeace hatchet job than a reasoned analysis of the science surrounding GM issues [and] aroused understandable outrage from this country's scientists." ... "This country's scientists?" Perhaps [A. P.] means all with the exception of the 14 scientists on the panel ... including [one] at the University of Guelph ... apparently "academic freedom" at that university allows trashing of your colleague's work in non-peer reviewed journals.

The article in question was co-authored with a visiting Irish journalism student now employed in a similar capacity at the CFIA.

The assistant professor profiled above for denigrating the quality of the Royal Society of Canada's Panel on the Future of Food Biotechnology also authored the quote that began this article. Charging that scientists have failed in their responsibility to teach students to "think critically and provide well-informed decisions"—given the compelling evidence marshalled by the Royal Society of Canada panel—offers a particularly transparent example of doublespeak.

Conclusion: What Is Education For?

In his provocative text *Earth in Mind,* educator David Orr of Oberlin College asks, "What is education for?" He notes that the various crises confronting the world today—ranging from global warming to shrinking biodiversity—are not the work of ignorant people. He refers to a similar observation from Elie Wiesel, who noted that the perpetrators of the Holocaust were the heirs of Kant and Goethe, among the best-educated people on the planet.

Wiesel's explanation of "what went wrong" in Nazi Germany bears repeating in the context of academic doublespeak today. Wiesel stated that the education of pre–World War II Germany "emphasized *theories* instead of values, *concepts* rather than human beings, *abstraction* rather than consciousness, *answers* instead of questions, *ideology and efficiency* rather than conscience" (Wiesel, 1990).

Has our curriculum today been informed and nourished by this insight? When academics commit themselves to proprietary research of no apparent redeeming social value, meanwhile teaching students how to discredit detractors through doublespeak, what *values* are we bequeathing to the future? Are students learning critical thought processes leading to meaningful questions, or are they rewarded for the speed with which they can parrot answers lifted from the electronic media? Teaching "content" in isolation from "context" and "product" independent of "process" has placed us perilously close to the values of Orwell's *1984.* Unless and until academics acknowledge that doublespeak has no place in academia—let alone society—regardless of how many overhead dollars it brings in, we cannot hope to step back from the precipice that awaits us, and our students.

Part III

Brave New Workplace

6

Beware the Campus CEO
Donald C. Savage

University professors should be concerned when presidents or rectors start calling themselves CEOs. This title strongly suggests that they have bought into a view of the university as little different from a private sector business. Their purpose is to produce graduates with narrow training for particular jobs at minimum cost and to perform cheap research for the private sector. In this vision, students are outputs and faculty are employees, as in any other business. Management techniques can then be applied to the educational process. Some universities have already have gone through all the fads—Total Quality Management, Management by Objectives, Management by Walking Around, and the latest, Performance Indicators. These strategies are designed to increase management power, reduce faculty influence, and cut costs, particularly salaries and benefits. In Canada, these presidents/CEOs want to roll back the governance of universities to the autocratic patterns that were the norm before the 1960s, although now the patterns are dressed up in fancy new managerial language.

This radical shift in philosophy has had a profound effect on the academic freedom of professors and on the quality of life within the university. The last twenty years have been the age of the accountants and the bureaucrats, although the performance indicators of accountants has left something to be desired of late. Individual professors are subject to much more control and bureaucratic reporting has increased dramatically, hand in hand with advances in the electronic world. Since most faculty are their own administrative secretaries, such demands cut significantly into research and teaching time. Whatever can be counted is counted. Whatever can be micromanaged from the top is micromanaged from the top.

These developments have occurred all over the world but particularly in the United States, the United Kingdom, Australia, New Zealand, and Canada. For many years New Zealand was touted as the laboratory for the application of these ideas, and, as a consequence, it is worth paying some attention to the events in that country.[1]

The New Zealand Experiment
In the late 1980s and 1990s in New Zealand, the most extreme ideas met little opposition because of the political landscape in that country. For most of its history New Zealand, like Canada, had first-past-the-post elections, but there were no checks or balances in the constitution. New Zealand was a completely unitary state with no functional upper house like Australia's, no provinces like Canada's, and no check on a majority government other than the possibility of losing the next election. In the 1980s, the governing Labour Party was converted to a right-wing vision of society. The opposition National (conservative) Party merely said that the government had not gone far enough, and when it came to power in 1990, it proceeded to up the ante. As a consequence, the priests of the counter-revolution felt free to express fully what they wanted to do, since they were certain they were going to win. The new vision was laid out for all to see in great detail, even though, in the end, the vision was not fully realized. The events in New Zealand should be of interest to academics in Canada, where there is a tendency to cloak these matters in soothing words and to promote incrementalism in the university world rather than the blitzkrieg.

In 1997 the New Zealand Business Round Table, in a submission to the government, stated that education was not a right and that the argument for universal education was a Marxist notion derived from the 1936 Soviet constitution. As for universities, it wrote: "Tertiary education is an economic product like any other."[2]

Key partners with the government in promoting the new order were the international accounting firms, particularly Ernst and Young and PricewaterhouseCoopers. Expressions of their common vision can be found in the parliamentary debates, the Green and White Papers of the National Party government, the reports commissioned by the government from the accounting firms, submissions of the Business Round Table, and the like.[3]

To the accounting companies, faculty and students were the enemy. They characterized faculty in the debate as a selfish interest group only interested in high pay and short hours, unlike other honest hard-working New Zealanders. Students were freeloaders on the state who should as soon as possible be made to pay the full cost of their education. The accounting companies put forward a picture of themselves as above the fray, giving disinterested advice to the government so that New Zealand could proceed to a perfect free market in the university world.

It was important, so it was argued, to reduce the power of special interest groups such as faculty and students by banning them from boards of governors and by eliminating the decision-making powers of academic councils or any such body other than the board of governors. This argument was a subset of a more general attack the government was waging on trade unions and the laws that guaranteed their rights. The attack on collegiality continued through the 1990s. The current Labour government, elected in 1999, is less dogmatic than its predecessor and has commissioned a report on university governance that recommends more collegial structures.[4] Whether the government will act on it remains to be seen.

In accordance with the government's wish to cut taxes and dramatically prune the scope of government, one of the first acts of the National Party when it came to power was to convene a meeting with the vice-chancellors, in which they were lectured on the importance of cutting salary and benefit costs.

The National Party wished to promote private universities in competition with the existing state-financed ones. Throughout the 1990s there was a running debate on how to correct what was perceived as the unfair position of the publicly funded universities in the higher education market. This correction could be achieved, so the purists suggested, through an annual capital tax on university assets that would eventually through them down to the financial level of polytechnics or the private providers in one equal higher education market. The proponents said that the plan was designed to ensure the efficient use of space.

In the best of all possible worlds, universities would be privatized and required to show a profit. The preferred model would be private companies that could be bought and sold in the free market. In the meantime, the minister of education should be the sole shareholder and thus the owner of the universities, nominator of boards of governors, author of mission statements, and the like. Privatized universities would dispense with unions and could selectively rehire academic staff of their choosing.[5]

One of the more dramatic proposals suggested that the minister, rather than subsidizing the universities, should purchase individual student outputs from them or anybody else. The minister would contract for targeted education and training courses, with the course content being specified by the minister. The minister could focus on practical courses and the taxpayer would not have to pay for the trivial programs in the humanities and social sciences or esoteric ones in science and mathematics.[6]

This is why there was such a vigorous debate in New Zealand in the 1990s over who owned the universities. It seems a bit arcane to Canadian ears, but it was crucial to the implementation of the neoconservative vision. If the government owns the universities, it can do as it pleases in terms of governance and management. The universities would be no different from a government department. If not, it has to proceed either indirectly by financial manipulation or directly by legislation, thereby allowing much more debate.[7]

In this vision the clause in the Education Act requiring academic freedom in the universities was a barrier to the free market. So too were the clauses defining the universities, in part, as the critic and conscience of society and as institutions that undertook research. These functions were externalities that could not be costed and should be abolished.

The new corporate university would demand loyalty and obedience on the part of its employees, including the faculty, just as in any other private enterprise. Public pronouncements and speeches would be vetted to ensure that the brand name of the university was not adversely affected. No one would be allowed to criticize the university in public. This trend was more pronounced in Australia than in New Zealand, perhaps because the most spectacular case in New Zealand involved a right-wing academic, Dr. Martin Lally. Dr. Lally thought that New Zealand universities in general and his in particular had not advanced in the direction of the market economy nearly fast enough and wasted their money on politically correct enthusiasms. He said so frequently, vigorously, and publicly. Should he be punished in the same manner as left-wing critics of the status quo? Speech codes sometimes come back to haunt those who set them up.[8]

One of the favourite demands of finance departments in thrall to neo-conservatism is to insist on the separation of teaching and research. This demand also appeared in New Zealand, where it was hoped that university research could be transferred to crown corporations that would allow government to dictate the nature of the research and the professional standards involved. In turn, this demand would have meant that the universities would become, in practice, merely a few additional years of secondary school. The prestige and influence of their faculties would correspondingly decline, making it much easier politically to cut salaries and benefits and to substitute part-time for full-time academics. The current Labour government has maintained the distinction between research and teaching by creating a national competitive funding mechanism for research, not restricted to the universities, and another structure to measure and to reward successful teaching. The rest of the vision is in limbo.

One of the oddities of the right-wing revolution in New Zealand and in the United Kingdom is that zealots dedicated to the abolition of government as much as possible could end up advocating highly centralized systems of control and insisting that the government owned the universities. This approach in turn required massive bureaucratic structures and much more reporting and the counting of everything in sight. Even Margaret Thatcher eventually said that she had never intended such a centralized and dehumanizing bureaucracy, but by that time it was too late in the United Kingdom.[9] Many critics on the right also announced that they were defenders of high academic standards, but the neo-conservative revolution in New Zealand and the United Kingdom has been a triumph of philistinism.

Saved by the Ballot
However, in New Zealand the local politics changed with the arrival of a new voting system in the mid-1990s. This practice was similar to the German system, which combined first-past-the-post constituencies with other members elected according to party lists. After the subsequent election the National Party had to seek a coalition in order to form the government. The consequence was that blitzkrieg techniques were impossible and that extreme ideology would be more difficult to implant, particularly by legislation. As a result, many of the ideas noted above did not come to fruition, although they remain to reappear another day if the circumstances allow it. The National Party government had to content itself with Green and White Papers and with debate over mechanisms of quality assurance. New Zealanders voted for the Labour Party in 2000—a party that had shed a good deal of the right-wing vision it embraced so enthusiastically in the 1980s. The party, however, inherited a bureaucracy zealously committed to the new order and, like its counterpart in the United Kingdom, still tempted by micromanagement. It therefore remains to be seen how it will all turn out.

The extremism of the neo-conservative proposals in New Zealand ensured that vice-chancellors as well as the academic staff opposed them. It is important that academic staff work with liberal administrators to resist these trends. Unfortunately, both administrators and academic staff can be seduced by neo-conservative rhetoric into thinking that the new order is inevitable or at the very least efficient, when it is neither. The rhetoric is especially seductive for administrators because it promises virtually unlimited power even though in the end that promise, as demonstrated in New Zealand, is false as well, since real power flows to the bureaucracy. The vice-chancellors are left to do the dirty work.

Given half a chance the neo-conservatives in Canada would attempt elements of the same scenario as in New Zealand. After all, the guru of the New Zealand government in the 1980s was a Canadian, Roger Douglas, who lectured in this country on the virtues of the new order and the importance of blitzkrieg tactics to put it in place and to destroy the opposition.

Canadians might also want to note the role of the international accounting firms in the attack on faculty and students in the university system in New Zealand. It is ironic that North American accounting firms, which operate across the globe, have turned out to be the facilitators of corporate graft and crony capitalism on a scale that can only provoke wonder in the university community, whether in Canada or New Zealand, where graft and corruption in the university are extremely rare.[10] Furthermore, these firms and their allies are fighting hard in the United States and Canada to avoid the type of regulation that they proposed for the universities in New Zealand. We find the chairman and CEO of Ernst and Young, David Leslie, telling the Canadian Club in Toronto that "Overreaction resulting in over-regulation is a very real danger…. It could drive down quality, and complying with regulations is a costly burden on business." "You can't regulate trust," he said. Outside bodies, he suggested, cannot fix things through rules and laws. The only process that works is self-reform by individual companies, perhaps guided by a non-binding ethical framework that would encourage honesty and integrity.[11] And what has the university community been saying to the Thatcherite regulators and micromanagers for the last two decades? "Enter the inquisition, exit loyalty."[12] Perhaps the right hand in the accounting world should occasionally talk to the left hand. Then the university might be a happier workplace.

7

The One-Note Chorus
Frances Russell

In 1997, James Winter, professor of journalism at the University of Windsor, published a book on the perils of a suborned media. Its title is as arresting as it is true: *Democracy's Oxygen: How Corporations Control the News*. Professor Winter argues that just as life forms cannot breathe and will die without oxygen, democracy cannot breathe and will die without the oxygen of a free media.[1]

Corporate power over media used in pursuit of its special interest poses as much threat to freedom of the press as government power does. Conglomerates, media chains, media convergence, media monopolies—all are threatening, limiting, and frequently choking off oxygen to free and informed debate and opinion.

Yet the problems in journalism go far beyond media ownership. Yes, journalists feel a chill. But more than that, many, perhaps a majority, see nothing wrong with today's economic/political power construct and think fellow journalists who do are simply "leftists" or "conspiracy theorists."

Two illustrations leap readily to mind. Although the conference leading to articles in this book occurred in the nation's capital, within a stone's throw of Parliament Hill, a major media centre, none of the major media bothered to cover it. Could it be that was because it had the word "dissent" in its name? That it was sponsored by "unions"? Both these words are a red flashing light to many journalists today.

At the *Winnipeg Free Press*, the legislature beat used to be considered the top job in the newsroom, something a journalist had to work up to over a period of years. More recently, of course, it isn't. The new "stars" are those who write entertainment, sports, and business columns. But before things shifted, during Manitoba's previous provincial Conservative administration, a "star" arrived and went out to cover a ministerial news conference. He returned to the press gallery and immediately sat down to write his story. When asked if he had sought out the opposition parties for reaction, he was astounded. "Why would I bother?" he said. "All they do is criticize."

To adapt Noam Chomsky's phrase, consent has already been manufactured—and as much if not more so within the journalistic community as in the public at large.

To understand why Canada's media is shutting down opportunities for dissent and diversity, it's vital that we first examine what is happening to democracy. If democracy is polluted and degraded, so also will be the media.

Government of, by, and for the Elite
Government has been corrupted by the global shift to corporatism—government of, by, and for corporations and not citizens. The media, the means of communication and control in modern mass societies, have played a key role in the takeover.

Beginning in the mid-1990s, Ekos Research, the respected public opinion research firm, launched a multi-year intensive examination of Canadians' attitudes. Entitled "Rethinking Government," it continues to this day and is now the most in-depth and largest study ever of the dynamics of Canadian society.[2] It shows there is an enormous attitudinal and value gulf between the elite and the street. This, in itself, is not surprising. What is surprising and alarming is the fact that the elite, making up less than 20 percent of the population, almost always gets its way. The other 80 percent are systemically ignored, dismissed, devalued, overridden.

Other public opinion surveys support Ekos's findings. Consider the facts: In poll after poll, the public says it prefers investment in public goods such as health and education to balancing the budget, paying down the debt, and cutting taxes.[3] Governments of all political stripes and at all levels provide what? Balanced budgets, debt repayment, and a seeming relentless drive to ever-lower taxes.

Canada's elite insiders, Ekos says, not only seek to shrink government back to its nineteenth-century vestige through balanced budgets and ever-lower taxes but are also determined to integrate Canada with the United States, replace medicare with for-profit medicine, eliminate the social safety net, and decentralize, privatize, deregulate, and corporatize virtually all public services. They favour increased government spending in only one area: the defence department, with its lucrative contracts for business.

These messages dominate all mainstream media all the time. Editorial opinion and commentary is similarly monolithic in advancing them as if they are immutable laws of nature, unchallengeable. TINA—There Is No Alternative—we are told ad nauseam.

Remarkably, however, throughout the entire high-water period of the neo-conservative revolution of the 1980s and 1990s, Canadians in majority never wavered in their attachment to state activism. Ekos reported they wanted governments to create jobs, educate the young, provide health care, and look after the needy. They saw decentralization as a stalking horse for the weakening of government and a threat to publicly accountable institutions and services. They worried about creeping Americanization. Although their concern about the deficit did rise thanks to the incessant hullabaloo from the elites and their mouthpieces in the media, about half believed the issue had been manufactured by the elite to justify winding down government.

But if the public was tuning out the elite/media message, politicians were not. Whether nominally left, centre, or right, all governments sang from the neo-conservative songbook and delivered the elite-insider wish list, from free trade to deficit reduction to tax cuts to the shredding of the social safety net.

Governments are all afraid of the lash of elite fury, the cutting off of investment, the ripping away of jobs, and perhaps most important, the relentless ragging and insults of right-wing editorialists, commentators, and radio and television talk show hosts.

Little wonder Canada posted the lowest voter turnout among the major western democracies save the US by the time the 2000 federal election rolled around. We've all heard the cynicism among our friends: You vote, but nothing changes. What's the point? They're all the same.

In one of my first interviews with him, Ekos president Frank Graves said the gulf in values and power between the elite and ordinary citizens is creating a crisis of political legitimacy. "All governments, regardless of political stripe, look remarkably similar. It's a plausible part of the public's anger,"[4] he said.

Stated the 1995 Ekos report:

> There is evidence in Canada of relative discontent with the narrow and unsuccessful pursuit of prosperity and competitiveness.... This neo-conservative agenda still seems to be a powerful force in the elite world of government and business. The huge gap separating the world of elite and public governance values is a crucial challenge for rebuilding the basic legitimacy and public responsiveness of government.[5]

This was a titanic clash, indeed, going to the very heart of our understanding of democracy and to its meaningful survival; a clash a free and democratic media should have leaped to cover exhaustively and extensively. Instead, the media was *parti pris*—not only a charter member of the elite-insider group but its chief proselytizer. With very few exceptions, Ekos's findings were totally ignored.

Nothing Free about Free Trade

The key turning point in the corporatization of the Canadian media occurred in the 1988 so-called "free trade" election. Although a majority of Canadians voted for parties opposed to the trade deal, only three newspapers—the *Toronto Star*, the *Edmonton Journal*, and the *Montreal Gazette*—spoke out against it on their editorial pages. And in the case of the *Gazette*, the publisher countered the editor with a pro–free trade column on page one.

Editorials are one thing. The news is supposed to be something else again. But this time, even that pretense to fairness and balance was abandoned. The news coverage of the election was heavily biased in favour of the trade deal. One newspaper even went so far as to feature headlines like "Turner's Lies" and "Broadbent's Deceit" above its masthead and pointed to its commentary page, employing the exact same epithets being hurled by the Tories and the Business Council on National Issues at the pact's political opponents.

The news coverage in most of the Canadian media changed from partial to laughable during the recession that struck the Canadian economy once the pact was signed. In the frenzied search for so-called "balance," every job lost and plant closed had to be matched with a job created and plant opened, even if the reality was usually closer to fifty closed or lost to one created or opened.

After that, it seemed, free trade died and went to heaven. It is hardly ever mentioned except in effusive puff pieces heralding Canada's enormous and ever-growing trade with the United States. The revolutionary impact of that trade on our society, our environment, our economic, social, and cultural independence is referred to only now and then in a ho-hum, well-what-did-you-expect way, one or two sentences buried in a rush of superlatives about our economic growth rate. It is almost never cited as a plausible reason for the dramatic widening of the gulf between rich and poor, the large increase in homelessness and use of food banks, and the hollowing out of our corporate sector, productivity, and competitiveness.

We've all heard the old saw that dog bites man is not news but man bites dog is. Even that has gone by the boards in much of today's corporate media. Day after day, the nation's newspapers are festooned with identical repetitive headlines about this corporate executive or that right-wing think tank warning about the disaster of deficits, the horror of debt, the "unaffordability" of medicare, the urgent need to adopt the American dollar, the incompetence and venality of public institutions as opposed to the brilliance and creativity of the private sector. Broken records, all. But stories about the vast and negative changes in our society are buried, if they are published at all, on the back pages.

I am very pessimistic. I see no easy answers to the disciplining of dissent in the media. By focusing only on trying to fix the media, we are dealing with a symptom. The solution can only come with confronting the fundamental problem—corporatism. The media, after all, is a reflection of its society and carries all its flaws. It cannot remain open when society itself is being closed down.

A first step is to remove the power and influence of money from politics. Manitoba and Quebec have done so. In the dying days of his prime ministership, Jean Chrétien brought in limited controls on corporate and union donations, but due to a pitched battle within his own party, the legislation is mere baby steps. Much more urgently needs to be done. Political parties that have to go out onto the highways and byways of the nation and raise their money from real people—perhaps by stooping to selling fudge, as Tory backroomer Norman Atkins once said in horror—will be more likely to listen to us ordinary folk. Politicians who have to raise money solely from their citizens and not the ever-ready multinationals might be more willing to look at the ancient recommendations on media ownership and concentration from the Davey Commission of the early 1970s (shelved) and the Kent Commission of the 1980s (also shelved). They might also be more open to the idea of a newspaper CBC, or an arm's length news equivalent of the Canada Council to fund local newspaper and radio and TV co-operatives.

Press Freedom for the Chosen Few
Journalists of a left-wing, and sometimes even centrist, persuasion have suffered career dead ends and dismissals ever since those political terms were first used. Their fates went unnoticed and unmourned. In the bygone era of many newspapers and local owners with a sole interest in publishing, at least some could find alternative employment.

But today's corporate and absentee ownership by giant transnationals who see media as little more than the propaganda arm for the rest of the oligopoly is not so benign. Certainly, Russell Mills's patron and friend Conrad Black made a point of getting rid of journalists with whom he disagreed, often slagging them publicly to boot.

Mills lost his job as publisher of the *Ottawa Citizen* after running a feature critical of the Prime Minister and an editorial calling for his resignation. He claimed the owners, the Asper family of Winnipeg, told him after the fact that he should have submitted the pieces for approval. Mills was quoted in a CBC interview: "I had no way of knowing that was their expectation. They've given many guarantees about the editorial independence of the newspapers to the CRTC [Canadian Radio-Television and Telecommunications Commission], to the Heritage committee of the House of Commons."[6]

I believe the Mills imbroglio tends to tarnish the whole noble battle for freedom of the press. Mills became a press freedom hero because he alone among the legions of the persecuted was a member in good standing of Ekos's elite-insider group. He was felled, supposedly, by government, not a corporation.

In his 1998 book *Yesterday's News: Why Canada's Daily Newspapers Are Failing Us,* John Miller gives us a real look at Mills based on a personal interview.[7] When Black purchased Southam's chain of newspapers, Mills flew to New York to present him with an ambitious plan to turn the *Ottawa Citizen* into a paper that would be respected, as he put it, "among the people who are significant to him, who are people in the high levels of government and business." That meant, in Miller's words, a new, more conservative editorial policy. Back in Ottawa, the dirty work happened quickly. *Citizen* editor Jim Travers was offered another job. The paper's editorial page editor, Peter Calamai, winner of three national newspaper awards, citations from UNESCO, and a Michener Award, was fired.

Continues Miller, "Within weeks, the *Citizen*'s editorial policy changed … there was a friendlier line towards the Mike Harris government. Mills cleaned out his editorial board and replaced it with writers, some of them non-journalists, whose resumés spoke of work for the far-right Fraser Institute and the Harris government." Mr. Calamai's replacement was William Watson, a conservative economist whose last column for the *Financial Post* said history should judge former Prime Minister Brian Mulroney to be a great Prime Minister.

"I'm making sure that the things that are published in the *Citizen* are things that I personally agree with," Mr. Mills said in that book interview. "I have to be able to defend them because Conrad may be on the phone saying, 'Why did you do that?…'"

The only surprising thing about the furor over Mills's firing by the Aspers was that anyone, particularly any journalist, was surprised. After all, we journalists surely know that owner influence over newspapers is as old as the printing press. In countries like Canada and the United States with written constitutions that include a bill of rights, press freedom is part of the freedom of speech clause. As a senior executive of CanWest Global explained to me, freedom of speech belongs to those with the power of speech—that is, those who own the printing press or the broadcast network, not the scribes they hire.

There was an interesting follow-up to the Mills story in my hometown of Winnipeg. Lesley Hughes, a well-known Winnipeg journalist, had her freelance column with the *Winnipeg Sun* summarily terminated because she was out of sync with the arch-conservative views of its new owners, the Toronto-based Sun Newspaper Group. During the 1999 Pan-American Games in Winnipeg she had written several articles chastising the *Sun* for its high-profile attacks on Cuba. She appealed her peremptory dismissal to the Manitoba Human Rights Commission and received a $1,000 compensation payment from the *Sun*.

After the Mills firing, CBC Winnipeg Radio's noontime Questionnaire phone-in show featured Hughes and the *Citizen*'s ex-publisher. Hughes asked Mills if he was as concerned about corporate influence and censorship in the media as he was about government influence and censorship. Mills tersely replied he was not and furthermore had no intention of even discussing it.

Mills's response says it all. Mills is not a poster boy for press freedom. He is a symbol of press corporatization.

Handmaids to Power
Nor is Mills alone. Instead of being critics and challengers of power, journalists have become handmaids to power. Few are prepared to acknowledge that real power has long since shifted from the political arena to the corporate world; from the accountable political forums of city councils, provincial legislatures, and Parliament to the unaccountable closed-door world of globalized business, finance, and currency traders.

We are all fiddling while Rome burns. Compared with the machinations around the Canadian dollar, Lawrence McAulay's patronage peccadilloes pale. Yet try to find just one story that details, let alone criticizes, the daily cynical futures trading on national currencies while economies and millions of lives hang in the balance.

Could it be that journalists earn too much? After all, we are among the most empowered and wealthy members of society. We identify with elite interests because we are charter members of the elite; our jobs, promotions—yes, our egos—depend on advancing their interests, not reflecting the opinions of the general public, let alone the dispossessed. Very few are left who chart their careers by the adage that the journalist's role is to afflict the comfortable and comfort the afflicted.

Finally and perhaps most important, an alarmingly large number of journalists know little of Canadian history or understand our political institutions. If there's no collective memory, no understanding of Canada and how and why its institutions and values differ from those of the United States, for example, how can we discharge our role to give Canadians the information they need to fulfill their role as citizens?

8

Dissent May Not Need to be Disciplined: Corporate Influence in the News Media

Robert A. Hackett

I'm in an odd situation: As an academic specializing in the study of journalism and news media, I should be at home writing about either media or academia for a book in which scholars and journalists are exploring common problems, such as diversity and defence of an independent public sphere. But in practice, I'm more comfortable discussing constraints on journalism than those in my own institution (cf. Hackett, 1991).

Why? We don't like to urinate in our own backyard; there's little incentive to engage in critical reflection on our own occupational practice—and that's the first clue to how dissent is constrained. Notwithstanding their claims to the unbiased pursuit of truth, reflexivity is not really encouraged within media or academic organizations.

The question "How is dissent disciplined?" requires us to define dissent. I propose understanding it as peaceful, reasoned challenges to current policies or leadership (reformist) or even to fundamental assumptions or values (revolutionary).

These challenges may target the institutions where we work. They may be directed to key client or sponsor institutions: in the case of media, these could be advertisers or the state; for universities, they might be the state (public funding) or corporate funders of internships, employment, research, or chairs (which might help to explain, for example, why we do not hear more vigorous critiques from more Canadian journalism schools about media concentration). Or challengers might take aim at broader dominant political, cultural, and economic interests—for example, the ideology and policies of market liberalism, or consumerism, or (especially in the United States) militarism.

If we assume the expression of such dissent is healthy in a democracy and is part of the "best practice" of both media and academia, is it under threat today? Much discussion has focused, rightly, on the aftermath of 9/11 and the potential for a new McCarthyism. There have been cases of outright censorship or intimidation of both journalists and academics. In the fall of 2002, I identified some of the subsequent blind spots in 9/11 coverage (Hackett, 2001b):

- Why did 9/11 happen?

- What are the policy options apart from massive military retaliation?

- Was 9/11 a case of "blowback" from forces that had been unleashed in part by US foreign policy?

- Who is the enemy in the so-called "war on terrorism"? How far do the targets extend? What counts as a victory?

- What's the state of public opinion outside the United States?

- Could the vicious attacks of 9/11 really be considered "Islamic" terrorism?

- What political agendas are piggybacking on the response to 9/11?

- How are civil rights being eroded?

- Is G. W. Bush the legitimate commander-in-chief, or was his election engineered through fraud in Florida?

- How are civilian casualties in Afghanistan justifiable? Is the actual conduct of the war defensible?

There was a real post-9/11 chill, one that made these highly relevant questions difficult to raise in the public forum. But that chill affected the United States more than Canada; media more than academia; TV more than print media; Arab or Muslim minorities arguably more than dominant culture.

In any event, we shouldn't obsess on 9/11, or on overt cases of censorship and intimidation. These are important, to be sure. But US media weren't bastions of diversity or critical thought on September 10, 2001. Constraints are more structural than exceptional; more implicit than explicit; more embedded in than opposed to institutional norms and professional ethos (for instance, "objectivity"); more carrots than sticks.

More often than not, dissent doesn't need to be disciplined; through institutional procedures and socialization, its expression is pre-empted in the first place.

Influences on the Media

To help make this point, I'm going to turn to Shoemaker and Reese's (1996) model of factors or pressures that influence the selection and framing of news. They identify five "layers" of influences, a hierarchical model that starts with the most immediate workaday level and moves "outside" from there.

The first level comprises media workers, or *journalists*, themselves. Their conceptions of their professional roles and ethics are said to have a direct influence on content, whereas their socio-demographic backgrounds and their personal and political beliefs shape news indirectly, especially when individuals can exert power to override institutional pressures or organizational routines (Shoemaker & Reese, 1996, p. 65).

Daily *work routines* in the newsroom are the second level. For instance, news is typically obtained through routinized "beats," which may be focused on topic areas (science, the economy) but more often on institutions capable of generating an efficient and predictably newsworthy supply of material—Parliament, city hall, the courts, and so forth. Further dimensions of news routinization include standardized genres (soft/hard news, reports, features, columns, editorials, etc.) and the key news agencies like Canadian Press, which editors use to guide the selection process. This aspect of news production was well captured colloquially by a Canadian actor in a skit from the old TV variety show *Hee Haw*. That program may not have been television's crowning achievement, but Don Herron's quote rings true: "The news today is the same as it was yesterday, it just happened to different people." And in the era of saturation spectacles like the O. J. Simpson and Monica Lewinsky scandals, even the characters are fairly constant.

The third layer of influence is found in the broader *organizational imperatives* of media institutions. Here, the profit orientation shared by private media companies, combined with their hierarchical structure, in general shape content in accordance with ownership's interests. Considerations of supply, production, and consumption translate into maintaining a steady and manageable supply of news, efficiently producing it, and presenting it in formats that attract profitable audiences. The media corporation needs both to maintain credibility with its public, and to make profits. (Shoemaker & Reese, 1996, pp. 105–137; Hackett & Gruneau, 2000, pp. 34–35).

The fourth layer comprises *extra-media influences*, including institutional sources, advertisers, the political power of governments, market structures, the legal framework, and technology.

Finally, and most broadly, is the *influence of ideology*—a system of values and beliefs that governs what we see as "natural" or "obvious" and that serves in part to maintain prevailing relations of power (Shoemaker & Reese, 1996, pp. 221–224). This includes the interplay of social relations, cultural narratives, and power structures at the societal level. Ideology not only shapes news; it is extended, renewed, and reproduced through media content.

Reviewing this model, it is important to note that news is not primarily a product of journalists. Although they are on the front lines of daily production, newsworkers' autonomy is constrained by the

Dissent May Not Need to be Disciplined

organizational context within which they work. If I had to choose the dominant factors that shape the news today, they would include the structured dependence on official and institutional sources not only for information but for a sense of what counts as news (Gans, 1980); the commercial imperative of attracting affluent consumers whose attention can be sold to advertisers (Smythe, 1981); and the strategies of cross-promotion and rationalization within corporate empires that own more and more of North America's largest media and that increasingly dominate global markets (McChesney, 1999).

Shoemaker and Reese's hierarchical model identifies a broad range of determinants, and it is a useful antidote to reductionist explanations of the news as the product of some single factor. Nevertheless, it is noteworthy that the corporate and class interests of the socially privileged operate at every level.

Journalists

To the extent that journalists are influenced by their social circles outside the workplace, it is surely significant that senior editorial decision makers and opinion columnists tend to be affluent, upper-middle-class boomers. An interesting research project by Vancouver journalism students in 1993 revealed that the value of houses owned by thirteen top managers and columnists at the *Vancouver Sun* averaged $413,000, far above the city-wide average at the time (Roberts, 1993, p. 30). In a classic study of elite power in Canada, sociologist Wallace Clement (1975, pp. 283–284) argued, borrowing from Max Weber, that there is a process of "elective affinity" in the news media, one which:

> ... expresses the way ideas and material interests "seek each other out" in the ongoing processes of society.... It involves the selective perception of previously generated ideas to suit the current position of the actors.... In the study of mass media, this can apply to those who are in the situation of selecting from available information what they consider to be "news" and to frame that information in a context which suits their view of the world.... In this way there is a built-in conservatism in the impact of the media by tending to reinforce whatever presently

exists. The propensity to accept any given information depends upon the ability to fit it into an existing framework and equally important, the previous evaluation of the source of the information.

As noted above, journalists' notions of professionalism are probably more important than their social background or their strictly personal values in influencing how they approach their work. It has been argued that the doctrines of professionalism taught in journalism schools and on the job lead journalists to internalize commercial and corporate imperatives (McChesney, 1999, pp. 49–50). Take for instance the concept of "objectivity," which at first sight has a very democratic premise: that information should be available to all, without fear or favour, and without distortion by vested interests. But the practical utility of objectivity in the emerging commercial daily press of the nineteenth century was less altruistic; it can be traced to the emergence of mass markets and the desire of press proprietors to attract larger audiences and advertisers and to fend off the threat of government regulation as chains and monopolies grew apace. In practice, the ethos of objectivity leads journalists to over-rely on official sources and conventional wisdom (Hackett & Zhao, 1998). Objectivity in journalism (one suspects in academia too) has little to do with producing truth; it has a lot to do with producing what's safe and marketable.

According to Canadian journalists I have interviewed, as commercial imperatives extend their influence in the newsroom, a process of selective retention and promotion also influences content. Those journalists who are most apt to be dissenters are more likely than others to burn out or to move on to other careers, more so, I suspect, than academics, who often have more control over their work process and can bury themselves in their own projects.

Routines of News Corporations and Organizational Imperatives
The second and third levels of influence, the routines and organizational goals of news corporations, are ultimately determined by ownership, which allocates resources, hires senior personnel, determines target

markets, and sets broad policy guidelines. At some level, news content will register the organizational culture of the corporation within which it was produced, and that culture is management's responsibility.

Accordingly, it is relevant, and problematic, that in North America media, the family-owned firms of yesteryear have been displaced by conglomerates preoccupied with short-term profits and competitive strategies to attract target audiences and advertisers (Underwood, 1995). As news decision making is increasingly subordinated to these overriding concerns, the autonomy of journalists has eroded, and with it, the period of "high modernism" in North American journalism, symbolized by icons like TV newscaster Walter Cronkite, has ended (Hallin, 1996).

Extra-Media Influences
The fourth level, extra-media corporate influences on content, includes the needs of advertisers, who provide the daily press with about 75 percent of its revenues, and the publicity strategies of corporations and corporate-funded "free market" policy institutes as sources for news accounts.

Such institutions are well positioned to engage in "information subsidies"; that is, they can distribute expensively produced and newsworthy (but self-serving) information at virtually no cost to media (Gandy, 1982). One example of such an information subsidy is the annual "Tax Freedom Day," a research-based media stunt produced by the neo-liberal Fraser Institute to make the ideological point that too much of Canadians' income is collected and spent by government (Hackett & Zhao, 1998, p. 157). A less direct but broader corporate influence is the "gravitational pull" on the media by governments and political parties that in turn are tied structurally, socially, and ideologically to the corporate elite through party financing, interpersonal connections, and the dependence of the state on tax revenues derived from a capitalist economy (Clement, 1975; Winter, 1997).

It might seem that audiences are a counterweight to corporate influence on the media. The primary justification for the commercial media system is that of "consumer sovereignty"—the idea that the media respond effectively to consumer choice and thus "give people what they want." It conveys an image of unified and determined consumers barking orders to compliant media corporations, who then produce the programming that consumers want.

But there's a huge problem with this argument. In reality, many structural factors deflect or undermine the expression of consumer preferences in commercial media content. These factors include: high entry costs and oligopoly (the small number of competitors) in media markets; media owners' political interests, which can't be simply reduced to commercial considerations; the dispersion and diversity of media audiences, and the fact that audience power is limited to choosing from only those alternatives that are already available and profitable (Curran, 1996; Hackett, 2001a).

Above all, the consumer sovereignty argument ignores the crucial role of advertising. Economically, the commercial media's bread is buttered not by audiences as such, but by advertisers who pay for access to audiences of the right kind. Advertisers want to reach not just anyone, but those people most likely to buy their products—in particular, affluent people such as professionals, investors, and executives. The commercial media have an incentive to tailor their content to appeal to the cultural and political sensibilities of the affluent, sensibilities that on economic issues, tend to be conservative. Thus, affluent consumers have a disproportionate influence in determining what kinds of media content and media outlets will economically prosper and which ones will not even survive. The history of the British press has shown that progressive national dailies attracting millions of working-class readers went out of business while more conservative papers like the *Times* or *Daily Telegraph* flourished with much smaller, but upmarket, readerships (Curran, 1979).

In addition to its bias in favour of affluent audiences, there are other ways in which advertising has made the political content of commercial media more apolitical and more conservative than was the popular press of the 1800s. Considered historically and structurally, the emergence of the commercial mass press over a century ago had a number of implications for editorial content, including non-partisanship and depoliticization, as profit-oriented news organizations sought to avoid alienating portions of the intended audience. That did not mean the press was suddenly devoid of political stories or values; rather, such values "tended increasingly to be implicit and hegemonic (dominant and consensual), rather than explicit, abrasive, and partisan" (Hackett & Zhao, 1998, p. 67). The flipside of depoliticization was the promotion of consumerist lifestyles over other social values, like ecological sustainability, which might contradict the advertising messages. But again, political blandness does not mean neutrality; the spread of commercial logic in the press helped to marginalize progressive alternatives, partly because advertisers themselves "disliked liberal and radical-left views that might raise questions about the role of big business" (Bagdikian, 1997, pp. 129–130; Hackett & Zhao, 1998, pp. 68–69).

Indeed, according to Smythe (1981), commercial media's most important commodity is the audience itself—specialized audiences that correspond to a particular market niche for advertisers, or affluent audiences whose disposable income is especially attractive to advertisers, or mass audiences who can be appealed to with broadest-common-denominator content and whose individual lack of purchasing power is compensated by large numbers. It is this structure that gives affluent audiences more weight than less affluent ones (Hackett & Zhao, 1998, pp. 68–69).

The Influence of Ideology
At the fifth and broadest level of influences on news content, the ideological legitimacy of private capital, generally secure in a stable capitalist economy, is even further enhanced by the current cultural and political hegemony of free market fundamentalism (a.k.a. neoliberalism, market liberalism). Such hegemony was not a "natural" or spontaneous public response to government deficits resulting from out-of-control social spending. Although the emergence of market liberal hegemony is too complex to analyze here, we can say that its preconditions included an ideological mobilization within the capitalist class in response to cultural and political challenges during the 1960s and 1970s to the very legitimacy of corporate capitalism, against a background of the declining rate of profits globally, with the end of the long-term postwar boom and the OPEC oil price shock of

1973. Increasingly, the capitalist class took on the project of unravelling the postwar welfare state consensus and rolling back the social security net. The elections of Thatcher and Reagan in 1979 and 1980 respectively were political landmarks in this process; less dramatically and somewhat later, the 1984 MacDonald Royal Commission's endorsement of free trade with the United States marked a decisive shift in the orientation of Canada's corporate elite. In this neo-liberal project, which consciously targeted public opinion and the media as well as policy makers, corporate-funded "think tanks" like the C. D. Howe and Fraser Institutes played key roles (Carroll & Shaw, 2001). Likewise, corporations in the media and communication sectors, far from being neutral observers, have been "the new missionaries of global capitalism"—active ideological and political proponents, and economic beneficiaries, of the neo-liberal project (Herman & McChesney, 1997).

I have outlined a set of pressures on the media that might be expected to result in a skewed, class-biased picture of the world. Research conducted since 1993 by NewsWatch Canada, a media monitoring project at Simon Fraser University, has identified systematic "blind spots" and double standards that we believe reflect this view. Several examples follow in the next section.

Content Patterns in the News

Patterns of selection and omission are even more consequential for setting the public agenda than are apparent bias or double standards in the topics reported. That is, what is *not* covered may be more important than *how* news is covered. The NewsWatch research suggests that relative to their public significance, the following topics have been under-reported in Canada's press: labour news; alternatives to the neo-liberal approach to economic policy; white-collar and corporate crime; religion and traditional social values; poverty and class inequality; the power of the public relations industry; the extent of Canada's involvement in militarism and its negative consequences; and the vested interests of corporate media themselves (Hackett & Gruneau, 2000, pp. 165–216).

Labour and Business

About three-quarters of Canadians are employees—workers—or dependants of workers; many of them are members of trade unions, organizations intended to advance their collective economic interests. The proportion of Canadians who derive their income solely from ownership of capital, or who actively monitor their investments, is much smaller.

The proverbial visitor from Mars would hardly be aware of these realities from Canada's daily press. In Hackett and Gruneau (2000, pp. 194–195), we reported that in the *Vancouver Sun* in 1997, business received much more coverage than labour and was more likely to receive upbeat or positive coverage. Labour sources were much more likely to be counterbalanced by opposing sources than were business spokespeople. Furthermore, business appeared in a range of contexts, while almost half of labour news concerned strikes or contract negotiations. A follow-up study in 1999 compared business and labour topics in the *Vancouver Sun* and the allegedly more liberal or pro-labour *Toronto Star*. Taking both papers together, not only did business receive much more overall coverage than labour, but business was three times more likely to receive positive coverage than negative. Labour, on the other hand, was twice as likely to receive negative coverage as positive. In the *Sun*'s general news section, of the total sources accessed in the sampled items, business spokespeople made up almost one-fifth of the "defining" sources—those whose views are consistent with the story's frame—compared with one-tenth for labour. In the *Star*'s news section, there were more labour- than business-defining sources. However, in the business section of both papers, labour was nearly absent as a defining source.

A case study of coverage by the three Toronto dailies of the 1996 protests against neo-liberal policies implemented by then Ontario Premier Mike Harris and his Conservative Party found that the newsworthiness of the protest lay in its disruption of public transit and other government services. The political significance of the demonstrations was covered, but it was marginalized by the overwhelming number of stories about the immediate and mundane inconveniences of the protest. The press focused on the involvement of organized labour, largely ignoring the extensive involvement of other social groups in the protest coalition, such as anti-poverty activists, artists, parents, or faith-based organizations. Also missing was much attention to the grievances and purposes underlying the protest (Hackett & Gruneau, 2000, pp. 196–197).

Alternatives to Neo-liberalism
As noted above, Canada's corporate elite since the 1980s has coalesced around the ideological project of neo-liberalism. Thus, one potential aspect of corporate influence in the press is the access accorded to neo-liberal policy institutes or "think tanks" compared with their rivals on the left of the political spectrum. A 1996 NewsWatch study of coverage of six right-wing (market liberal) and seven progressive policy institutes in twelve major daily newspapers and two television networks revealed a heavy weighting in favour of the right. The second stage of this study found the qualitative tone and style of coverage of the right-wing Fraser Institute and the left-wing Canadian Centre for Policy Alternatives (CCPA) to be similar. Quantitatively, though, the Fraser Institute had a more than five-to-one advantage over the CCPA in the *Vancouver Sun, Globe and Mail,* and the CBC and CTV national TV news (Hackett & Gruneau, 2000, pp. 204–205). In a second study, after the opening of the CCPA's Vancouver office the following year, the gap fell to 2.4 to 1 in the local daily, the *Sun*. However, certain qualitative differences were found. For example, the Fraser Institute was accessed in a wider range of topics and was six times as likely to have its research mentioned in news stories (Gutstein, 1998, pp. 9–10).

A very similar imbalance was noted in a study of seven dailies and their coverage of eight right-wing, seven left-wing, and four centrist policy institutes. The average number of media hits per institute was 38 for the right, 17.3 for the left, and 7.8 for the centre. Front-page coverage of the left and right institutes was almost even, but the right received much more main news section, business section, and op-ed page access than did the left.

"Elective affinity" expresses the way ideas and material interests "seek each other out" in the ongoing processes of society. It involves the selective perception of previously generated ideas to suit the current position of the actors. In the study of mass media, this principle can apply to those who are in the situation of selecting from available information what they consider to be "news" and framing that information in a context that suits their view of the world. In this way there is a built-in conservatism in the impact of the media, which tends to reinforce whatever presently exists. The propensity to accept any given information depends upon the ability to fit it into an existing framework and, equally important, the previous evaluation of the source of the information.

Is the imbalance noted in these studies due to the "elective affinity" between editorial decision makers in the corporate press and right-wing institutes? Or is it a function of the sheer output generated by the right? To address this question, the researchers asked the various institutes to estimate the volume of their public releases during the sample period. This information yielded a ratio of media hits to public releases of slightly more than 4 to 1 for the left, slightly less than 4 to 1 for the right, and about 2.5 to 1 for the centre. In other words, a left institute's press release has as much chance of generating a media hit as does its right-wing counterpart. These findings suggest that if indeed there is an active discrimination by the press, it is apparently against centrist institutes whose output is perhaps less provocative and therefore less newsworthy.

Nevertheless, the sheer access to corporate resources that enables the free market think tanks to produce the highest ongoing volume of reports and releases itself generates inequalities in the public agenda. According to some normative models, a democratic press in a stratified society has an obligation to counteract such imbalance consciously; otherwise, the media will unwittingly favour inequality (McChesney, 1999, p. 288). However, there is evidence that the conservative perspectives are favoured in the news quite apart from the access accorded to policy institutes as such. For example, NewsWatch found that in a three-month sample of the *Globe and Mail* in 1994–95, neo-liberal solutions to the deficit (cutting social program spending, downsizing government, reducing provincial transfer payments, privatizing public services) were mentioned more than three times as often as progressive alternatives (government spending to stimulate the economy, lowered interest rates, reduced subsidies or higher taxes for corporations) (Mosdell, 1997).

This result does not seem to square with the conventional notion that journalists, and therefore journalism, are biased in favour of "left-liberal" causes. What is one to make of this apparent contradiction?

First, the "left-liberal bias" thesis rests on the assumption that news is essentially a product of working journalists, a view that the Shoemaker and Reese (1996, pp. 63–103) review of the relevant literature refutes or, at the very least, sharply qualifies.

Second, journalists in any event are hardly raving radicals. Writing in what at the time was one of Conrad Black's more independent-minded dailies (*Edmonton Journal,* November 10, 1996), former diplomat Harry Sterling challenged Black's views of journalists as irresponsibly leftist:

> We fail to detect many journalists in Canada who could qualify for the label of leftists by traditional standards … Perhaps by "left" Black means those who collectively stumble over each other in their eagerness to support every politically correct cause or motherhood issue while ignoring the real forces shaping society. However, these journalists represent no serious threat to those who control the real levers of power. Admittedly, they occasionally go through the motions of appearing to challenge the establishment, nipping a few ankles, but this in turn helps propagate the illusion that the press and media are not beholden to anyone. But if critical journalists were as radical as portrayed, they'd be demanding a higher progressive income tax, an end to tax shelters, and nationalization of profit-loaded banks and petroleum companies. But they don't. (Cited in Hackett & Gruneau, 2000, p. 226)

Still, no myth works unless it has some purchase on reality. There is indeed a watchdog tradition in the media, a stance of speaking for "the little guy" against entrenched interests. That stance has certainly not disappeared, and it has led to news stories that have angered or embarrassed corporate leaders. But since the 1970s, investigative journalism has declined; when it does appear, typically it is directed not against the corporate elite but against particular politicians or "safe" targets representing less powerful interests, such as "lax" refugee or parole boards or fraudulent welfare claimants (Hackett & Zhao, 1998, pp. 49–50).

To be sure, on social/moral issues, such as abortion, gay rights, and gun control, journalists may well have "liberal" views. Nearly thirty years ago, two Canadian political scientists pointed to an uneasy accommodation between the secular, urban, socially liberal views of many journalists and the economically conservative interests of media owners. It is as if journalists are given latitude to express liberal views on social or moral questions so long as they do not fundamentally or repeatedly challenge the core political and economic interests of media owners and the rest of the corporate elite (Hackett & Gruneau, 2000, p. 225).

Despite all these qualifications, the concept of the "left liberal media" persists, partly because it is itself part of the market liberal ideological offensive, heavily promoted by think tanks like the Center for Media and Public Affairs in Washington, DC, and a parallel project in Canada, the Fraser Institute's National Media Archive. It is of course a very useful myth, because it implies that the media need to move even further to the right in order to become more balanced.

White-Collar and Corporate Crime
Although white-collar and corporate crime has social consequences as severe as violent crime in terms of workplace deaths and economic losses, the former types of crime typically receive far less news attention (Hackett & Gruneau, 2000, pp. 182–184). This observation is not to imply absolute contrasts; the news agenda can shift, and in 2002 some spectacular corporate bankruptcies in the United States put corporate crime temporarily in the media and political spotlight. This observation is to suggest, rather, that this kind of crime has been under-reported for years and has to meet higher thresholds of impact before it becomes newsworthy.

Poverty and Growing Class Inequality
If a "corporate agenda" or class bias influences the news media, one aspect of that would be a relative lack of attention to the problems

facing the poor, or even to the very fact of poverty. A comparison of the *Vancouver Sun* in 1987 and 1997 found that coverage of poverty decreased in comparison with other topics despite an increase in poverty during the same period, and framing of the poor became somewhat more critical or distancing. Although most stories still portrayed the poor sympathetically, there was evidence of a notable increase in news that portrayed them as threatening. There was also a decline in the use of advocacy groups for the poor as sources, and an increase in business and government sources (Hackett & Gruneau, 2000, pp. 199–201).

Advertising Influence
Advertiser influence can be considered corporate influence because of both the internal profit imperative of commercial news outlets to attract revenues and the external expectations of advertisers and advertising firms, which tend to be large corporations themselves. The influence of advertisers may take the form of direct pressure (Soley, 2002), but more typically it takes more subtle forms, such as self-censorship or the allocation of newsroom resources. In terms of content, advertising influence may be manifest in several ways. Editors may avoid or minimize negative coverage of particular advertisers or general business interests, a phenomenon more likely to occur at small-market papers or those dependent on a single advertiser and less likely at metropolitan dailies with diverse advertisers and relatively well-trained and professional journalistic staffs. Conversely, content in small-market publications may include "advertorials" or news items designed to promote particular commodities or companies, such as specialized newspaper sections tailor-made for particular advertisers (for instance, Travel, Wheels, New Homes, etc.). More generally, the editorial environment may be conducive to putting audiences in a "buying frame of mind," and most broadly and crucially, to selecting content that is intended to attract commercially profitable audiences.

Other Blind Spots
The NewsWatch research has also suggested other significant public issues that receive relatively little press coverage: the extent of Canada's

involvement in the international arms trade and the negative consequences of militarism; environmental degradation as a systemic and ongoing problem; the perspective of non-Quebecois francophones in Canada's national unity debates; the influence of religion and traditional social values; and the influence of lobbyists and public relations firms in setting political and media agendas (Hackett & Gruneau, 2000, chapter 6). Arguably one of the most significant blind spots concerns media coverage of their own industry. We have found that newspapers tend to be less critical of their parent companies than papers with outside ownership; that newspapers tend to downplay the media industry as a political interest group; and that their editorial stance, ultimately determined by ownership, influences their news coverage.

Overall, many of these double standards or patterns of omission related to politics and class tend broadly to be consistent with what one would expect from corporate and commercial pressures. Commentators occasionally misread the NewsWatch research as informed by some form of conspiracy theory (Miller, 2001) or, at the very least, as wedded to a radical instrumentalist conception of news as "the product of the biases, motivations, or manipulations of ... politically conservative media elites" (Hackett, 1991, pp. 60–61). Neither is the case. Although we have a particular interest in examining the extent of corporate pressures on the news, nowhere do we claim that these are the only important determinants. The corporate sector itself is not a unitary and all-powerful force; like other social actors, it is both subject to, and participates in, the (re)constitution of structured social relations.

The corporate sector, however, does have more material and ideological resources than most other social groups. It is probable that pluralism in Canada's press system significantly depends on the degree of ideological pluralism within the corporate elite and of structural pluralism in media ownership. At a time of relative ideological cohesion around market liberalism within economic and policy elites, and convergence and concentration within the media system, those safeguards are now arguably in jeopardy (Hackett & Uzelman, 2002).

Disciplining Dissent

Finding Common Cause

That doesn't mean that no diversity or dissent exists or that media are an entirely closed system—far from it. There are fissures and contradictory tendencies within the media system—between ownership politics and media organizations' need for credibility with audiences, for example—and there are spaces within the surrounding political culture that have been opened up by determined individuals and groups, whether journalists or social advocacy groups and marginalized voices, such as women and gays. And since the end of the Cold War, there is arguably more scope for critical columnists.

In some ways, the system demands diversity. Too much homogeneity would be commercially unprofitable. Whether in universities or news organizations, dissenters and gadflies offer a convenient political screen for media owners and university administrators—proof that they are open-minded and inclusive.

Two conclusions follow from the arguments in this chapter.

First, dissent within contemporary corporate news organizations generally does not have to be overtly disciplined, because its expression is curtailed in the first place. A set of limits to public discourse—broad, flexible, and negotiable, but limits nevertheless—becomes normalized and routinized in newsroom operations, and to some extent internalized by journalists themselves. From assumptions about what topics are newsworthy and which sources are credible to the location of beats, the allocation of resources, and the criteria for promotion, contemporary journalism has institutionalized pressures toward conformity.

A second conclusion is that the pressures faced by journalists are not unlike those faced by academics, as described in other chapters in this book. It is a logic of the corporate enclosure of the public commons of knowledge—partly through copyright and intellectual property regimes and through the commodification of knowledge—that increasingly, access to information becomes dependent on the ability to pay. In both institutions, we see a strong shift toward profit centres and catering to the affluent at the expense of the principle of universal access—whether to education or to relevant civic information. Perhaps academia has not yet reached the point of many newsrooms, where journalists are encouraged to think of themselves as corporate team players through managerial concepts like "total newspapering" (Underwood, 1995). But examples from elsewhere in this book suggest that universities are hardly immune to corporate and commercial pressures, with implications for the casualization of the workforce and the production and dissemination of knowledge. So if journalists and academics face similar pressures, perhaps they have a common interest in preserving an independent public sphere.

To be sure, the two groups have rather different occupational cultures. Both professions seem to be engaged in very similar enterprise: truth-seeking in the public interest. But we conduct our work according to different professional codes, narrative conventions, and epistemologies, with academics in many disciplines searching for abstract generalizations, and journalists accustomed to individual-focused stories. According to one of my former students, a very perceptive newspaper writer, journalists often dismiss my own field, media studies, partly because we are telling a different story about journalism than the one they like to tell about themselves.

Nevertheless, this book is an encouraging sign that it is possible for journalists and academics to find common ground. The next tasks are to define concrete campaigns and objectives in order to make collaboration politically meaningful, and to reach out to other potential partners, librarians and schoolteachers seemingly the most obvious, with a direct stake in preserving democratic public access to knowledge and in building a movement for communicative democracy (Hackett, 2000).

Part IV

Policing Dissent: The New Chill on Campus and in the Newsroom

9

Students and the Fight for Free Speech in Canada
Ian Boyko

Anti-terrorism legislation and the growing police crackdown on dissent and protest threaten to erode civil liberties in Canada and abroad. What is the significance of these developments and how do they affect journalists and academics?

The state's relationship with universities has always, by definition, been rife with tensions, not least because the university is a social institution that requires vast funds to operate without adhering to traditional measures of productivity, and because faculty and students are (and should be) vocal critics of society, and therefore, government. Most of the measures used against protests and dissent on campuses are intended to curb embarrassment for political ends rather than to promote security and public safety.

Policing Dissent
We have seen a particularly ferocious policing of dissent used against the so-called anti-globalization movement. This movement is unfairly and inaccurately traced back in the mainstream press to Seattle 1999. I will begin as far back as 1997, to start with a pivotal Canadian example of the policing of dissent.

Disciplining Dissent

The APEC (Asian-Pacific Economic Co-operation) Conference protests at the University of British Columbia in 1997 saw the unethical and illegal pre-emptive arrest of activist Jaggi Singh. Singh was apparently one of the agreed upon leaders of the demonstration for the visit of pre-eminent human rights abuser President Suharto of Indonesia. It would later come out, rather unabashedly I might add, that Singh and others were arrested to curb the "embarrassment" of President Suharto.

Another example that hit particularly close to home for me because I was studying in Windsor at the time, was the policing measures used for the Organisation of American States (OAS) meeting in June 2001. Along the same lines as Jaggi's pre-emptive arrest, RCMP officers visited the homes of several local activists under the auspices of friendly introductions. These "introductions" were obviously meant as an intimidation tactic, to say: "We know you are a trouble-maker, and we know where you live."

Another pre-emptive measure undertaken by police was the direction given to the University of Windsor's conference services to cancel all of the non-campus bookings in the co-managed student centre. It wasn't difficult to re-establish the bookings under the name of the student union, but so much for the University of Windsor's community service mandate.

In addition to its complicity in shutting down the free speech of community and campus activists through attempting to eliminate space for discussion, the university was also complicit in the militarization of campus for the duration of the OAS meetings. Over five-hundred RCMP officers called the university's residence their home for a week. These same officers—the ones who would later be wearing helmets, holding shields, and wielding truncheons—also found the time to take strolls through campus in their free time wearing their firearms. Let's for argument's sake call it an armed patrol of campus. To me, it didn't feel like my campus was a space for free and open debate.

The police presence also extended to formal surveillance. We later found out that a psychology computer laboratory was cleared out for the week of the OAS meetings to accommodate police who were monitoring the Graduate Students' Society pub and offices across the street, where most of the puppet making, free-food preparation, and non-violent resistance training were taking place.

This policing of dissent also took on an even more abhorrent and personal face for me when my close friend was arrested in front of a high school distributing flyers about a demonstration opposing the OAS and the Free Trade Area of the Americas (FTAA). For this act of dissent, my fellow activist was held on a mischief charge in a temporary holding facility built for the protests that more resembled a dog kennel than a jail. As with most trumped up charges, they were later dropped when the OAS leaders and the media spotlight were both long gone.

But perhaps the most disappointing moment came later, when the senior administration of the University of Windsor was confronted by the graduate and undergraduate student unions about the police presence on campus during the OAS meetings. President Ross Paul and the vice-president of student affairs, John Corlett, were dismissive of the idea that a heavy, sometimes armed, police presence had disturbed the campus culture. In fact, they treated us as sore losers; the "other side" had as much right to be on campus as "our side," they said. Of course, this naïve position, frequently taken up by mainstream media, ignores the role of the police and/or military. Treating the police as if they occupied some space in a debate with fair trade activists borders on the absurd and turns a blind eye to the real job of riot squads, which is to do everything *but* debate. Perhaps recognizing this fact, Mr. Corlett reminded us on the way out that students in other countries are sometimes shot by police. None of us got shot that week, so I guess we are more fortunate than the poor students Mr. Corlett described.

Activists have even been targeted for simply criticizing the Prime Minister. When Memorial University of Newfoundland gave notice that Jean Chrétien would be receiving an honorary degree, the Canadian Federation of Students put out a news release to remind the Newfoundland public of Chrétien's lacklustre record on federal funding for post-secondary institutions; the students' union on campus planned a demonstration for the "degree"-granting ceremony; and the RCMP gave all parties a call to inquire further about the plans for dissent.

At one of Canada's most active campuses, Concordia University, the administration has been particularly heavy-handed in its limitations of the freedom to dissent. Following the emotional protests leading up to a scheduled talk by former Prime Minister of Israel Benjamin Netanyahu, a "cooling off" period was imposed. This measure prohibited any campus group or individual from holding politically related events.[1]

On October 16, 2002, shortly after a board of governors meeting to discuss lifting the moratorium, Concordia Students' Union vice-president Yves Engler was arrested for setting up an anti-FTAA table in a campus mezzanine. At the time of his arrest, Montreal police sent nineteen squad cars and riot police to the Hall Building and closed off Mackay Street. A police-enforced moratorium on free speech at a Canadian university did raise some eyebrows in the mainstream press and was condemned by the Canadian Federation of Students, the Canadian Association of University Teachers, and a few members of parliament, including the New Democratic Party education critic Libby Davies (Vancouver East) and Svend Robinson (NDP, Burnaby-Douglas). The ban was lifted before its planned expiry date.

An issue related to the policing of dissent is the militarization of Canadian campuses. Rather than showing a decrease in the presence of the military on campus, the trend seems to be heading in the opposite direction, including the use of on-campus recruiting. Given the previous examples of the police/military's relationship to dissenters and the role of the police/military as the deployment of the state's monopoly on "legitimate" force, military recruiting on campus is antithetical to the university's mandate to foster an open learning environment. For that reason, some student unions are banning military recruiting from student-owned space. The most recent ban was enacted by the University of Windsor Students' Alliance.

Disciplining and Discrediting Dissent
In addition to the outright policing of dissent, some universities and governments are able to control dissent through the less abusive, but equally effective, use of discipline.

Codes of student conduct, already in place at many Canadian universities, target students because by and large we are not protected by collective agreements. These codes go beyond the reach of the Criminal

Code and above reasonable academic standards, linking academic penalty to non-academic behaviour. They can link students' activism to their transcripts, as the code does at the University of Toronto.[2] Many student activists have already been threatened with the University of Toronto Code, and some suspect that a precedent was set last year when a marginalized activist was expelled. The case was fairly extreme, but the use of the code was specific and can be used in the future to stifle dissent.

At the University of Ottawa, a similar prohibition to the one issued at Concordia was established. The mandate was equally clear (from policy on the use of the Jock Turcot University Centre):[3]

PROHIBITED ACTIVITIES
11. A User shall not carry out activities in the University Centre which, in the opinion of the University,

a do not comply with this Policy;

b promote hatred, violence, propaganda or are of a political nature designed to disparage a government, state, country, religion, individual or group of people;

c harm the University's reputation or place the University in the middle of ethnic or other world conflicts;

d advertise or promote the sale of alcohol, tobacco products or illegal drugs;

e advertise or promote services or products that compete with the University's services or products or which contravene exclusive agreements between the University and a third party;

f result in the unwanted solicitation of the University's community or those visiting the University Centre;

g result in complaints or legal proceeding

I want to draw attention to three things outlined in this policy. First, prohibited activities include activities of a "political nature" that happen to disparage a government, which presumably includes Canada. Second, criticizing a government is equated with bigotry. Third, the University of Ottawa is clearly beyond criticism. Academic freedom in this context is muzzled in the most overt terms possible: Thou shalt not criticize the Establishment in our publicly funded space at the University of Ottawa.

I want to end on an example of disciplining dissent that cuts to the very heart of our rights as a democratically organized student movement. In British Columbia, the provincial government has made it very clear that it intends to "review" the legislation that enshrines a student society's ability to collect fees from its members. Our version of the Rand Formula is under attack. The provincial government has already abandoned legally binding contracts such as collective agreements for college instructors. We should expect the same treatment as an equally effective critic of the BC Liberals. The political precedent hanging in the balance is momentous, and I know that we can count on the labour movement to stand beside us in this fight.

Implications for the University
Public universities are funded by the public to operate in the public interest. Inherent in the notion of tenure is the freedom to offer a critical voice. If campuses cannot be counted on as a space for debate and protest, we are in danger of losing one of the most important foundations of democracy—free speech. Indeed, the entire raison d'être of public education institutions is critical thought. If public policy cannot be shaped by the open and honest discussion of competing ideas, then we are on the way to totalitarianism.

Given the role of free expression in a democratic society, students and faculty must see themselves as part of a larger movement—a movement that affords all people our "academic freedom" because free speech should be not only protected but also extended. In the words of David Noble, co-founder of the National Coalition for Universities in the Public Interest, "if we don't exercise it, we don't deserve it." Academic freedom is not a privilege, it is a responsibility.

10

Dissent and Collective Action in Oppressive Times

Aidan White

Journalists and teachers have much in common. As information professionals, we have an interest in protecting freedom of expression. We defend press freedom and academic freedom because they represent key elements of democracy.

But our respect for traditional values of professionalism in media and education is often the reason journalists and teachers come under pressure from governments and private institutions that want to control and manipulate the work we do.

Just how much we have in common was brought home to me a few years ago in Algeria, when the International Federation of Journalists (IFJ) opened up a crisis centre to help journalists, many of whom were being brutally targeted by extremists. We were not alone. A campaign of terror by religious and political extremists was directed against key professional groups—lawyers, journalists, and teachers. Why? Because of their role in shaping the moral and cultural values of society.

To journalists, our freedoms—in particular, freedom of expression and opinion—are fundamental to notions of quality and ethical conduct. The same is certainly true for teachers. We are natural dissenters, opposed by nature to political censorship or excessive commercial exploitation and committed to our right to act according to conscience. We oppose the presidents and ministers of information, the high-rolling advertisers and big-shot media owners who try to manipulate and control information for their purposes. Information is public property and should be gathered, shaped, and distributed according to sound ethical principles and made accessible to everyone.

In recent years the defence of this point of view has become more of a struggle. Over the past ten years, more than one thousand journalists and media staff have been killed and thousands more injured or jailed because they refused to submit to censorship.[1] At the same time, the growth of media monopolies on a national and global scale has cut deep into the culture of pluralism and free expression, upon which notions of democracy are based.

The Rise of Media Concentration
The political punch of concentrated media is powerful today and it is felt everywhere around the world. In Canada, the arrogant face of corporate media is shown by CanWest, the heir to the traditions of Southam, the country's largest newspaper chain. With its newspapers and television stations the company has access to about 97 percent of English-speaking Canada. The company's introduction of an editorial policy requiring its metro newspapers to publish editorials sent by head office in Winnipeg is a body blow to independence in Canadian media and an echo of the actions of Mediaset, owned by Silvio Berlusconi, the Prime Minister and media magnate in Italy, which has a stranglehold on 90 percent of the country's broadcast media. These companies are among the enemies of press freedom when they use their power to diminish pluralism and diversity.[2]

In most of the developed world, the newspaper industry over the past thirty years has become more concentrated. I note that in Canada the number of independently owned daily newspapers is down to just 5 this year from 29 out of 107 in 1970. Ontario, which had 18 independent daily newspapers in 1970, has none today.[3]

Throughout the western world, diversity of opinion in newspapers is shrinking. Journalists who express dissident opinions on their company's policies, the Middle East, the war on terrorism, or the consensus of national politics are marginalized and censored. Disagreeing with company policy can cost your job. At the *Montreal Gazette,* for instance, journalists who challenged CanWest's editorial autocracy have been threatened with the sack. Yet in any civilized and democratic society, they would be applauded for what they are—defenders of free speech.[4]

Governments everywhere allow media monoliths to grow without paying attention to the implications for pluralism and the public interest. This concentration of power—just ten global media conglomerates and around fifty regional corporations control most of the information available in the world today—comes at a critical, difficult, and dangerous time.[5]

War on Terror and Pressure on Free Speech

With a war on terrorism and uncertainty in the public at large, people are hungry for informed, reliable, and timely sources of information.

The global climate of the 1990s—when foreign policy purported to be driven by humanitarian values and human rights, and globalization was presented as an effective route to development and prosperity—has been replaced by a new order of political unilateralism. The advent of the security state and mounting evidence of unprecedented corporate greed and corruption make a mockery of corporate social responsibility.

At a time when we need dissenters to balance the power of establishment elites and when we desperately need media to open up the debate and give voice to alternative opinions, those diverse voices are being silenced. It used to be that dissent was challenging, loud, and radical, but today even the most timid expressions of opposition to the mainstream political and corporate consensus are isolated, ignored, and marginalized.

As a result we have bland, uniform, consensus-based reporting that fails to give people alternative viewpoints. Coverage of the war on terrorism, for instance, where the economic and political elites are united on the core issues, is uncomfortably close to that found in authoritarian societies with limited formal press freedom and where political leaders dictate the news agenda.

The rigorous questioning and scrutiny of elected officials is a benchmark of democracy, but it seems that many journalists, particularly in the United States and Europe, have allowed their watchdog function to lapse. Media are increasingly locked into a corrupt status quo. This problem is particularly acute in a political environment like the United States, where electoral laws and campaign costs have made politics a fiefdom for the super wealthy. As a result, the link between corporate power and political policy is hardly reported.

The close relationship between the US oil establishment and the elaboration of current policy in Afghanistan, Iraq, and the Middle East by the White House is hardly reported because journalists slavishly rely on official sources of information. As a result, journalism poses no challenge to plutocracy but rather underpins the anti-democratic nature of current politics.

Going to war is a serious business. It is arguably the single most important decision any society can make. Yet what is most striking in the US news coverage following the September 11 attacks is that it has failed to promote a proper debate about whether or not to go to war. The media have ignored tough questions: Why is a military and essentially unilateralist approach the most effective? Why should the United States determine—as judge, jury, and executioner—who is a terrorist or terrorist sympathizer in this global war? What is the role of international law in monitoring and limiting the actions of the United States in its assumed role as the world's police officer?

There is a complete absence of comment on the role being played by powerful interests in the United States who benefit politically and economically by an unchecked war on terrorism. Any credible journalist would remark on that absence were the events taking place in Russia or China or Pakistan.

The determination of the US administration not to be blown off course leads to political acrobatics that remain unchallenged by the media. An invasion of Iraq because it might have weapons of mass destruction remains on track even after North Korea announces it already has nuclear weapons. With little more than a diplomatic shrug the United States keeps the focus on Baghdad, ignoring the opening of a new front in the horrifying bombing on Bali or the concerns raised when Chechen terrorists hold Russians hostage in a Moscow theatre.

Some, like Robert McChesney, say that US journalism has been almost propagandistic. Even veteran US anchorman Dan Rather was moved recently to complain that journalists have succumbed to self-censorship. What is most telling is that his confession was aired on the BBC instead of being given to US media.[6]

The failure of journalism and media at this time reminds us that, as George Orwell wrote in his unpublished introduction to *Animal Farm*, censorship in free societies is infinitely more sophisticated and thorough than in dictatorships because "unpopular ideas can be silenced, and inconvenient facts kept dark, without any need for an official ban."[7]

The bitter truth is that there is a tendency of media professionals to submit to the subtleties of self-censorship because it is too dangerous or too much of a sacrifice to challenge corporate or political power. For journalists to raise issues like these does not suppose opposition to the government. But it does underscore the need for justification and explanation so that policy and action are the result of deliberation, not manipulation.

Small wonder, then, that in this age of passivity and corporate censorship there are increasing threats to civil liberties. Following the September 11 attacks, the IFJ carried out a survey on the impact of the terrorist attacks on journalism and civil liberties. The report, to which journalists' groups in forty countries responded, reveals a fast-developing crisis for journalism and civil liberties.

The war on terrorism has created a dangerous situation in which journalists have become victims as well as key actors. This is war of a very different kind. There is no set piece military confrontation. There is no clearly defined enemy, no hard-and-fast objective, and no obvious point of conclusion. Inevitably, this "war" has created a pervasive atmosphere of parancia in which the spirit of press freedom and pluralism is fragile and vulnerable. It has also led to media casualties. The brutal killing of Daniel Pearl and nine other journalists in the Afghanistan conflict has come to symbolize the appalling consequences of September 11 for journalism and for freedom of expression.

War is never good news for journalists. Inevitably, there are media casualties and, as always, journalism becomes a battleground as governments on all sides seek to influence media coverage in their political and strategic interests.

All governments are keen to demonize the enemy, but media, and the journalists who work for them, need to resist the legitimate desire of politicians to win the propaganda battle in favour of the wider public interest in maintaining freedom of the press. The priority must always be the right to publish words and images—however unpalatable—that help people better understand the roots of conflict.

That task is becoming more difficult, because in the weeks and months after September 11, democratic states, particularly the European Union states and the United States, quickly formed a joint approach on counter-terrorism actions, including measures that undermine traditional standards of civil liberties. In joint meetings in December 2001 and June 2002, European and US officials sought to co-ordinate policy, drawing up agreed lists of terrorist groups. In just three months, the European Union had a common legal definition of terrorism, a list of suspects closely in line with Washington's, and more than $100 million in private assets frozen.

The European Council, representing fifteen nations, adopted a package of measures to "improve the European Union's response to terrorism." There is now more cross-border co-operation between police forces and a Europe-wide arrest warrant to prevent suspected terrorists from evading arrest by crossing the EU's largely unchecked internal borders. The EU-wide definition of "terrorism" threatens to include people taking part in violent demonstrations over globalization. The changes broaden the scope of what constitutes terrorism to include actions that "seriously affect" (rather than "seriously alter") the political, economic, or social structures of a country or "an international organization." The latter brings international organizations such as the World Trade Organization and the World Bank into the picture.[8]

Tony Bunyan, the editor of *Statewatch*, a civil liberties watchdog, summed up the concerns of many when he said, "Draconian measures to control political dissent only serve to undermine the very freedoms and democracies legislators say they are protecting."

In June 2002 the IFJ protested when the European Parliament agreed to allow member states to put telephone calls, e-mails, faxes, and Internet usage under official surveillance. This surveillance compromises data protection as well as the capacity of journalists to monitor the apparatus of state and to store information.

Such an amendment to policy would have been unthinkable before September 11. But politicians on both sides of the Atlantic are using public uncertainty and security concerns to undermine people's rights and liberties. The citizen's right to private space and for the press to investigate and scrutinize the authorities without intimidation are freedoms that distinguish democracies from authoritarian regimes, and they must not be given up lightly.

But they are being given up. In the United States, Congress moved rapidly to adopt repressive new immigration and wiretapping laws and other anti-terrorist measures, raising serious concerns about civil liberties. Arab-Americans have been harassed and attacked. Music has been censored. In Texas, the FBI shut down Arabic Web sites. In Baltimore, the *Sun* reported that anchors and even a weather forecaster at one TV station were required "to read messages conveying full support for the Bush administration's efforts against terrorism."[9]

The Bush administration has several times tried to curb or control the flow of news. This anti-democratic tendency met resistance, which demonstrated the country's solid democratic traditions. Media critics of President Bush, like Tom Gutting, city editor for the *Texas City Sun,* and Dan Guthrie, a columnist for the *Grants Pass Daily Courier* in Oregon, were fired.

From the first day of the US military's Operation Enduring Freedom in Afghanistan in October 2001, the Pentagon tried to exercise control over media. An exclusive government contract with the firm Space Imaging prevented the company from "selling, distributing, sharing or providing" pictures taken by the Ikonos civilian satellite to the media. News outlets were thus deprived showing pictures of the results of the US bombings taken by Ikonos, the most efficient of the civilian satellites.

Media were also targets and victims in the rush to legislate against terrorism. Limitations on press freedom imposed by the government include undermining the confidentiality of Internet messages. Internet monitoring was formalized by passing of the Patriot Act, allowing the FBI to install Carnivore surveillance software on any Internet service provider to monitor all e-mail messages and keep track of the Web surfing of people suspected of having contacts with a foreign power. To do this, the only permission needed is from a special legal entity whose activities are secret. The measures also include easing the rules surrounding phone tapping. As well as the invasion of individual privacy, this blank cheque given to the FBI threatens the confidentiality of journalists' sources.

The American Civil Liberties Union (ACLU) condemns the laws, warning that "Most Americans do not recognize that Congress has just passed a bill that would give the government expanded power to invade our privacy, imprison people without due process and punish dissent."

"The new legislation goes far beyond any powers conceivably necessary to fight terrorism in the United States," said Laura W. Murphy. "The long-term impact on basic freedoms in this legislation cannot be justified." "For immigrants," added Gregory T. Nojeim, associate director of the ACLU's Washington office, "this bill is a dramatic setback. It is unconscionable to detain immigrants who prove in a court of law that they are not terrorists and who win their deportation cases."

Other threats lurk. Certain elements in Washington have been trying for years to ban the use of encryption technology unless the government could be guaranteed a way to crack the code. But when encryption is outlawed, only outlaws will use encryption. Many fear that in the desperate search for security, the right to private speech, to engage in public discussion, and to do so anonymously will be drastically diminished and the Bill of Rights substantially weakened.

The problem this threat illustrates is that the war on terrorism is being fought on the back of strategies that promote fear, ignorance, and intolerance. Since September 11, 2001, the democratic states have been dangerously ambivalent about their commitment to citizens' rights and press freedom. Their actions have reinforced cynicism in autocratic regimes about Western commitment to fundamental rights, and, even worse, they have inspired a fresh round of media oppression in countries that routinely victimize and intimidate journalists.

Journalists and Teachers: A Coalition for Free Speech

Journalists should be among the first to question politicians who make quick-fix promises in the name of security, particularly when our ability to collect and store information, to protect sources of information, to carry out legitimate inquiry, and to be independent of the policing and security services are at risk.

I have considered wider threats to free speech and freedom of expression as they affect journalists. Teachers, too, know that integrity and professionalism in the use of information is essential to democracy. But how can academic freedom and the right of teachers to act according to conscience be recognized and protected unless they, like journalists, are able to work freely? And how is the battle for academic freedom and free speech won without the support of other groups within society?

It should be obvious to all that the common good of society depends upon the unrestrained search for knowledge and its free exposition. That is why academic freedom in schools and universities is essential. Teachers should not be hindered or impeded in any way by the management of schools or teaching institutions from exercising their legal rights as citizens, nor should they be victimized because they exercise such rights. Nor should the academic community be subject to any restraint over research, debate, or consideration of issues such as those under discussion in *Disciplining Dissent*.

These well-established principles for teachers are less well known within journalism, even though we are engaged in the struggle for similar rights of professional independence. Some journalists' unions have included professional clauses in collective agreements to ensure their professional rights. Much has been done on similar professional issues by teachers' unions and other groups. But, to date, there has been precious little sharing of information or discussion of how journalists and teachers can work together in pursuit of common or, at least, complementary values.

Journalists, like teachers, are entitled to freedom in carrying out research and in publishing the results; the freedom to report is of equal importance to the freedom to teach and to discuss; both teachers and journalists cherish the freedom to criticize and demand freedom from censorship, whether that censorship comes from inside or outside the profession.

Academic freedom, like journalistic freedom, does not require neutrality on the part of the individual. Rather, academic freedom, like professional, pluralist, and inclusive journalism, makes commitment possible.

With all of these rights come responsibilities. Just as journalists have to find ways of self-regulation that command respect both within journalism and within the community at large, so academic freedom carries with it the duty to ensure that research and teaching are based always on an honest search for knowledge.

Over the past ten years we have built up a network of supporting organizations in the fight for free expression, which means that today no journalist is brutalized, censored, or jailed without a worldwide response. The International Freedom of Expression Exchange (IFEX) brings together a range of partners with diverse interests whose common goal of establishing a culture of respect for free expression has created a powerful and influential coalition.

Similarly, the arguments for opening up a dialogue between journalists and teachers and exploring ways of working together on some of these issues are, I believe, unassailable.

The struggle for human rights and democracy and freedom in the use of and access to information should not always be fought according to the narrow professional agendas that mark out our separate and distinct roles in society. A failure to collaborate and to share resources in pursuit of our mutual objectives and values could, in the end, diminish our effectiveness on our own ground. Better co-operation at all levels could effectively reinforce both the fight for academic freedom and journalistic independence.

What we need is a network that will deal with attacks on dissenting views and individuals. We should form coalitions with civil society groups. We need courage to act beyond our narrow professional interests to foster examination of the attacks that are currently being waged against free expression and democratic rights. We must build solidarity around programs of action against suppression of alternative opinions.

We come from traditions founded on the assumption that openness and dialogue are necessary alternatives to the exercise of unaccountable power. In a world where political and corporate power have coalesced around a ruthless and exclusive vision of the future that excludes millions and where the liberties won by trade unionists and libertarians are being chipped away, we would be seriously negligent not to work together to build a joint platform on which to struggle for the protection of our rights.

Part V

Summing Up: Resolve and Respond

11

Historical Co-operation between Academics and Journalists
Jon Thompson

The central problem facing our two communities is the erosion of freedom of expression, especially the freedom to dissent. This erosion results from several related factors: growing corporate concentrations; growing corporate influences; and inadequate responses to consequences of these developments by media editors, academic administrators, journalists, and professors.

Several writers in *Disciplining Dissent* have described the effects of far-reaching corporate influences and given striking examples of the failings of individual managers and employees in the media as well as in the academy. However, notwithstanding their imperfections, universities and the media are vital to the public interest, and so our fundamental task is to identify ways to strengthen their integrity and independence.

At one level, the problem is not new. For instance, the Canadian Royal Commission on Newspapers (Kent Commission) reported its findings on the adverse consequences of media concentration two decades ago. The current extent of this concentration and its international scope are of course new, but we can still learn from the past.

The main lesson of history is that alliances and collective action are needed to contend with powerful forces and interests. At the present moment, I believe there is once again a basis for mutual support in our two communities that extends beyond their usual interdependencies—namely, that academics depend on journalists to explain and disseminate their work to the public at large, and to generate public support for further studies; and that journalists depend on academics for expertise and interpretation as well as to provide material to write about.

These interdependencies go back a long way. For instance, it was Voltaire, writing in the early eighteenth century as one of the first science journalists, who brought the work of Newton to the attention of the European public.[1] It was Eddington's promotional work among journalists that resulted in "Einstein" becoming a household word in 1919. Eddington raised funds for international observation (headed by himself and Dyson) of a solar eclipse, during which one of Einstein's predictions was successfully tested.[2]

Subsequently, academics began to appreciate that they needed journalists to help defend academic freedom. To cite very recent examples, continuing international media coverage played a significant role in helping to bring both the Olivieri and Healy cases in Toronto to favourable resolutions.[3] The effects of the coverage were not confined to the public attention attracted by stories in the newspapers and other media. There is also a wealth of experience in the journalistic community that played a role in these cases and can benefit the academic community in future.

To illustrate the wider effects, I would mention that the work of the Committee of Inquiry in the Olivieri case—the members of which were Patricia Baird, Jocelyn Downie, and myself—benefited from the media. As noted in our report:[4]

- the existence of a still somewhat free press and its ongoing attention to the issues led the University of Toronto, the Hospital for Sick Children and the pharmaceutical manufacturer Apotex Inc. to make public statements that (perhaps unintentionally) contained information to which we would not otherwise have had access—these organizations apparently felt a need to justify their actions on various occasions; and

- the members of the Committee of Inquiry have been under unrescinded warnings of legal actions since the outset of the inquiry in the fall of 1999, and in contending with these have been assisted by a very experienced libel lawyer. His skills were developed through serving as legal counsel for a major media organization. (This is a novel instance of technology transfer from the private sector to the academic community, that may be a harbinger of things to come.)

Aidan White of the International Federation of Journalists (IFJ) has advocated alliances among journalists, academics, and others. As already mentioned, this approach has been effective in the past and is likely key to progress in future. In order to illustrate the general point, a couple of historical examples from different times and political settings are worth mentioning.

The first example is from Paris in the 1820s, under the regime of King Charles X of the restored Bourbon monarchy. The reactionary policies of this regime resulted in leading scholars of history and politics, such as Victor Cousin and François Guizot, being removed from their university teaching posts along with several younger colleagues. These academics organized themselves around a newspaper, *Le Globe*, which had recently been founded by a typographer, Pierre Leroux. They used the newspaper as a basis for influencing public opinion toward ideas of liberal democracy. In July 1830, new draconian measures by Charles X, including severe press censorship, precipitated the overthrow of his regime. Guizot, and others he had influenced, subsequently came to lead key government ministries that began a transformation of French society. This reform included establishment of a nation-wide system of public education in accordance with a plan drafted for Guizot by Cousin.[5]

The second example is from Montreal in the 1950s, under the reactionary regime of Premier Maurice Duplessis. A group of academics, journalists, and union leaders organized themselves around a magazine, *Cité Libre*, and they led transformations, first of Quebec society, then of Canadian society. The academic Pierre Trudeau came to head the country, while the journalist René Lévesque came to head the province. We may not agree with everything they did—indeed, they didn't always agree with each other—but incontrovertibly, both advanced democracy and strengthened freedom of expression.

Although I don't suggest such examples can or should be replicated, I do suggest that the leadership of the Communications, Energy and Paperworkers Union of Canada (CEP) and the Canadian Association of University Teachers (CAUT) could establish the nucleus of an alliance among journalists, academics, and other trade unionists. Establishing an independent newspaper or magazine may now be impractical—we are thinly spread across a large and diverse country, and to be widely read, such a periodical would be prohibitively expensive. However, other devices, such as holding periodic meetings of officers and senior staff to plan actions, organizing conferences to foster co-operation and alliances, commissioning task forces on specific issues, and maintaining a dedicated Web site are quite feasible.

Despite recent erosions, academic freedom is much more firmly entrenched in Canada than journalistic freedom. Academics today are also, on average, better paid and have greater job security than journalists. This was not always the case. In the 1950s, professors were poorly paid, had lower social standing than many journalists, had no significant academic freedom, and had job security only in proportion to their docility.

An event in Winnipeg in 1958 precipitated a Canada-wide movement that over the next two and half decades transformed the Canadian academic world. The event was the summary dismissal of a professor of history who, by dissenting, had incurred the displeasure of his college president. The summary dismissal for dissent was itself no novelty—what was new was the extensive published report of the first CAUT committee of inquiry, which was effective in galvanizing academics across the country.[6]

CAUT and its local associations then began to adapt the approaches of industrial trade unions to the academic world. They had the advantage in the 1960s of a rising tide of national prosperity and rising demand for their services. In the 1970s and 1980s they consolidated and extended the progress of the 1960s by unionization of locals and by promotion of wide-ranging policies on working conditions, including academic freedom. In the process, academic freedom was made not only respectable but legally enforceable, and the pay and status of academics greatly increased along with their job security.

As other contributors have noted, professors, like journalists, are employees. Just as academics learned and benefited from the work of industrial unions, so also journalists might find useful models in the advances in the academic workplace. Thus, it may be useful to outline the main elements of CAUT's strategy:

- develop robust policies—on academic freedom and tenure, professional responsibilities, appointments, promotion, and dismissal, as well as on university autonomy and governance;

- promote these policies—not only with CAUT's own membership, but with their employers—to create both respectability of, and demand for, the policies;

- entrench the policies through collective bargaining at the local level; and

- train members in collective bargaining and political action.

Many journalists have collective bargaining rights, but their collective agreements do not have the policy robustness of collective agreements for university faculty members. Peter Murdoch and his colleagues in the CEP have undertaken a major policy development initiative. Their work forms the basis for negotiation of a wide range of terms and conditions of employment for journalists, including freedom of expression and due process in disputes with employers, paralleling the earlier developments in CAUT. Perhaps CAUT could help in promoting wider public appreciation and support for this CEP initiative.

For our part, we academics had barely arrived in the congenial state of secure academic freedom when developments like "globalization" began rolling the clock back. This process has led to erosion of the scope and authority of democratic national governments everywhere, except perhaps for that of the United States, but its democratic status is increasingly in doubt. In consequence, public financial support for universities has decreased, and dependence on corporate financial support has increased, creating many of the pressures described elsewhere in these proceedings.

Academic freedom is now more seriously at risk than it was a decade ago, and to defend it in the current environment, we academics will have to rely on journalistic freedom in addition to our own resources. More generally, freedom of the press is vital to all of our democratic rights and freedoms. Thus, we must co-operate to help journalists recover more freedom to dissent—for the wider public interest as well as our own.

About the Authors

Ian Boyko is in his third term as the national chairperson of the Canadian Federation of Students. He has served on the executive of the National Graduate Caucus of the Federation and on the Board of Directors in the Federation's Ontario wing. Ian Boyko has a bachelor's degree in psychology from the University of Windsor and is pursuing a master's degree in sociology at that same university.

The Canadian Federation of Students has been lobbying the federal and provincial governments on student issues since 1981. The Federation comprises over seventy college, university undergraduate, and university graduate students' unions from across Canada and has a combined membership of more than 450,000 students.

William Bruneau taught at the University of British Columbia from 1971 to 2003. He specializes in the history, politics, and theory of higher education. Bill was president of the UBC Faculty Association from 1992 to 1994 and president of the Canadian Association of University Teachers (CAUT) from 1996 to 1998.

He recently co-authored, with Donald Savage, *Counting Out the Scholars: How Performance Indicators Undermine Universities and Colleges*

(Toronto: Lorimer, 2002). He is a member of the editorial team for volumes 16–19 of the *Collected Papers of Bertrand Russell*.

E. Ann Clark teaches in the Department of Plant Agriculture at the University of Guelph, with specific interests in managed grasslands, organic agriculture, and risks of genetically modified crops. She offers four courses, has authored more than two-hundred publications, and is a frequent invited speaker at scholarly and producer conferences.

Robert A. Hackett has taught in the School of Communication at Simon Fraser University since 1984. Since 1993, he has co-directed NewsWatch Canada, a news media monitoring project based at SFU. In 1999, he joined the Board of the Cultural Environment Movement, the "liberating alternative."

He is the author of *News and Dissent: The Press and the Politics of Peace in Canada* (Norwood: Ablex, 1991); *Sustaining Democracy? Journalism and the Politics of Objectivity* (with Yuezhi Zhao, Toronto: Garamond, 1998); and *The Missing News: Filters and Blind Spots in Canada's Press* (with Richard Gruneau and Donald Gutstein, Timothy A. Gibson, and NewsWatch Canada, Toronto: Canadian Centre for Policy Alternatives/Garamond Press, 2000).

David Healy studied at University College Dublin and University of Cambridge. He is a Reader in Psychological Medicine at the University of Wales College of Medicine, a former Secretary of the British Association for Psychopharmacology, and author of over 120 peer-reviewed articles and twelve books, including *The Antidepressant Era* and *The Creation of Psychopharmacology* (Cambridge: Harvard University Press, 1998 and 2002); *The Psychopharmacologists*, volumes 1–3 (London: Chapman & Hall, 1996); and *Let Them Eat Prozac*, published in the CAUT Monographs Series (Toronto: Lorimer, 2003; and New York: New York University Press, 2004). He is also a visiting professor at the University of Toronto.

Robert Jensen teaches journalism at the University of Texas at Austin in the areas of media law, ethics, and politics. Before taking up an academic career, Jensen worked as a professional journalist for a decade. He is the author of *Citizens of the Empire: The Struggle to Claim Our Humanity* (San Francisco: City Lights, 2004) and *Writing Dissent: Taking Radical Ideas from the Margins to the Mainstream* (New York: Peter Lang, 2001), and co-author of *Pornography: The Production and Consumption of Inequality* (New York: Routledge, 1997).

Award-winning journalist **Richard Leitner** has been reporting on the Hamilton scene for the past seventeen years, during which time he has also led his workplace union. His coverage of the Taro dump controversy garnered national recognition, including a Michener Award citation for public-service journalism.

Patrick O'Neill is President of the Canadian Psychological Association. He gave a decade of service to the Academic Freedom and Tenure Committee of the Canadian Association of University Teachers, the last three as Chair. His primary area of research is ethical decision making.

Frances Russell was born in Winnipeg and graduated from the University of Manitoba with a degree in history and political science. A journalist since 1962, she has covered and commented on politics in three provinces and Ottawa, working for the *Winnipeg Tribune*, United Press International, the *Globe and Mail*, and the *Winnipeg Free Press* as well as freelancing for the *Toronto Star*, the *Edmonton Journal*, CBC Radio and TV, and *Time* magazine.

She is the author of two books: *Mistehay Sakahegan—The Great Lake: The Beauty and the Treachery of Lake Winnipeg* (Winnipeg: Heartland Associates, 2000), which won the Manitoba Historical Society's Margaret McWilliams Award for Popular History in 2000, and *The Canadian Crucible: Manitoba's Role in Canada's Great Divide* (Winnipeg: Heartland Associates, 2003), nominated for both the popular and scholarly history awards in the Manitoba Historical Society's Margaret McWilliams 2003 competition. She is married with one son and one grandchild and lives in Winnipeg.

Donald C. Savage was educated at the universities of McGill and London in modern history. He taught in various Canadian universities, then became Executive Director of CAUT (1973–97). He was a principal drafter of the first UNESCO statement on academic freedom (*UNESCO Recommendation Concerning the Status of Higher Education Teaching Personnel*), the author of a report on academic freedom in the universities of New Zealand, and the co-author with William Bruneau of *Counting Out the Scholars: The Case Against Performance Indicators in Higher Education* (Toronto: Lorimer, 2002). Most recently he has written a report for the ILO on tenure and academic freedom in a number of democratic countries. He is an adjunct professor of history at Concordia University.

Gillian Steward is a Calgary-based author and journalist. In 2001–02 she was Visiting Professor of Journalism at the University of Regina. Her work spans newspaper reporting, magazine writing, radio documentaries for CBC's *Ideas* series, and non-fiction writing. She is the co-author with Kevin Taft of *Clear Answers: The Economics and Politics of For-Profit Medicine* (Edmonton: Duval House, 2000), and *Public Bodies, Private Parts* (a report for the Parkland Institute, University of Alberta). As managing editor of the *Calgary Herald* (1987–1990), she was responsible for day-to-day news coverage and special investigative reports. Steward wrote "Klein the Chameleon," a study of Alberta Premier Ralph Klein's use of the media to achieve power for *The Trojan Horse* (Montreal: Black Rose Books, 1995). She also contributed "The Decline of the Daily Newspaper" to *Seeing Ourselves: Media Power and Policy in Canada* (Toronto: Harcourt Brace, 1996).

Jon Thompson is professor of mathematics at the University of New Brunswick. He chaired CAUT's Academic Freedom and Tenure Committee from 1985 to 1988. He chaired the independent committee of inquiry into the Olivieri case, 1999–2001.

James L. Turk is executive director of CAUT. He previously taught sociology at the University of Toronto and directed the Labour Studies Program at University College. He has also served as director of education for the Ontario Federation of Labour.

About the Authors

Jim edited *The Corporate Campus: Commercialization and the Dangers to Canada's Colleges and Universities* (Toronto: Lorimer, 2000). He is a member of the Executive and Board of the Canadian Centre for Policy Alternatives and a member of the Advisory Board for the Ontario Institute for Studies in Education/University of Toronto.

Aidan White is the General Secretary of the International Federation of Journalists. He was born in Ireland and educated in Ireland and the United Kingdom, where he learned his trade as a journalist. He joined the International Federation of Journalists from *The Guardian* in 1987. He has worked as a reporter, feature writer, sub-editor, and editorial manager for leading regional and national newspapers in Britain, is a former member of the British Press Council, and an active trades unionist. He consults internationally on press rights and journalistic ethics and has produced reports for UNESCO, the ILO, the UN Human Rights Commission, the Council of Europe, and the European Union.

Notes

Preface

1. American Civil Liberties Union, *Freedom Under Fire: Dissent in Post-9/11 America* (New York: ACLU, 2003). Accessed 11 March 2004 from: http://www.ACLU.org/SafeandFree/SafeandFree.cfm?ID=12581&c=206
2. A special report of the American Association of University Professors entitled "Academic Freedom and National Security in a Time of Crisis" gives a thorough review of American anti-terrorism initiatives and their implications for the academic world. It appeared in the Novermber-December 2003 issue of *Academe* and is available from: http://www.aaup.org/statements/REPORTS/911report.htm
3. Roch Tassé, *Security and the Anti-terrorism Agenda: Impacts on Rights, Freedoms and Democracy* (Ottawa: International Civil Liberties Monitoring Group, 2004).
4. Canadian Bar Association, "Submission on National Identity Card Proposal" (October 2003). Available from: http://www.cba.org/CBA/News/pdf/idcards_oct03.pdf
5. Federal Research Division, Library of Congress, *Nations Hospitable*

to Organized Crime and Terrorism (Washington, DC: Library of Congress, 2003), 147.
6. Ibid., 152.
7. James Winter, *Democracy's Oxygen* (Montreal: Black Rose Books, 1997).
8. Jon Thompson, Patricia Baird, and Jocelyn Downie, *The Olivieri Report* (Toronto: James Lorimer and Company, 2001).
9. David Healy, *Let Them Eat Prozac* (Toronto: James Lorimer and Company, 2003); David G. Kern, "The unexpected result of an investigation of an outbreak of occupational lung disease," *International Journal of Occupational Medicine and Environmental Health*, 4 (1998: 19–32) David Bollier, "Preserving the Academic Commons" (paper presented at the 89th Annual Meeting of the American Association of University Professors, Washington DC, June 2003). Accessed 11 March 2004 from: http://www.learcenter.org/images/event_uploads/BollierAAUP.pdf

Chapter 2

1. George W. Bush, White House news conference, 11 October 2001. Text available from http://www.whitehouse.gov/news/releases/2001/10/20011011-7-index.html
2. George W. Bush, O'Hare International Airport, Chicago, 27 September 2001. Text available from http://www.whitehouse.gov/news/releases/2001/09/20010927-1.html
3. "DoD News Briefing—Secretary Donald Rumsfeld and General Richard Myers," US Department of Defense News Transcript, 25 October 2001. Text available from http://usinfo.state.gov/regional/nea/sasia/afghan/text2001/1026dod.htm
4. Lawrence C. Soley, *Leasing the Ivory Tower: The Corporate Takeover of Academia* (Boston: South End Press, 1995); George Monbiot, "Silent Science–The Corporate Takeover of Universities," in *Captive State: The Corporate Takeover of Britain* (London: Macmillan, 2000).

Chapter 4

1. Unless otherwise noted, the source for what follows is either my

reportage for the *Stoney Creek News* or personal experiences.
2. John Anderson of McMaster University's Labour Studies program examined the deal's shortcomings in his report "Privatizing Water Treatment: The Hamilton Experience, January 1999." Philip later sold the contract to Enron subsidiary Azurix Corp., which in turn sold the contract to German-owned American Water Services Inc.
3. Brenda Elliott was shuffled out her position as Ontario environment minister only weeks after announcing the approval of the Taro dump. Her successor, Norm Sterling, dropped by a Greensville conservation area that Halloween to announce that the Harris government would uphold the EAB decision to turn down the quarry dump there.
4. Kate Barlow, "Province Approves Taro Dump: Lack of Public Hearing Angers Opposition Group," *Hamilton Spectator*, 20 July 1996.
5. City of Stoney Creek, *East Quarry Landfill Proposal Executive Summary*, 30 May 1995.
6. As detailed by Chuck Pautler, director the Ministry of the Environment's environmental assessment branch, in memos to Deputy Minister Judith Wright on 7 and 8 September 1995. The memos were obtained by SCRAP under Freedom of Information legislation.
7. Allen Fracassi's wedding party included Luciano Pietrorazio, leader of Hamilton's infamous Barton-Sherman gang, who in January 1992 pleaded guilty to conspiring to commit murder in a contract killing of a rival. According to former employee Michael Hilson, Fracassi affectionately referred to Pietrorazio as "Luch" and displayed a picture of his wedding party in his office. An insider who spoke to me on the condition of anonymity recounted that Pietrorazio visited employees' homes after inventory allegedly went missing from a Philip yard.
8. *Fifth Estate*, 26 March 1996.
9. Paul Palango, "Are Public and Private Institutions Defending, as Well as They Might, the Public Interest in the Region Of Hamilton-Wentworth?" speech given to the Women's Canadian Club of Hamilton, Hamilton ON, 17 April 1996.
10. The Municipal Act allows councils to go behind closed doors for legal, personnel, and land acquisition matters. Stoney Creek Mayor Anne Bain claimed the meetings were open to the public, although

they were never publicized. Minutes of the meeting were released in 1997 under order the Ontario's freedom of information and protection of privacy commissioner.

11 Rae Corelli, "Small but Dogged," *Maclean's,* 12 May 1997.
12 Elizabeth Kelly and Michael Dismatsek, "Profiles in Courage," *Hamilton Magazine,* Fall 1997.
13 Philip Services Corp., "Amended Preliminary Prospectus," 24 October 1997.
14 "Taro East Landfill Provisional Certificate of Approval No. A181008," Annual Report 1997, 30 June 1998.
15 Steve Arnold and Barbara Brown, "Cyanide Charge Rejected: Philip Says Taro Clean," *Hamilton Spectator,* 13 October 1998.
16 Environment Canada's approvals are given in 19 March 1997 and 20 March 1997 notices headed "Letters To Proceed (Importation)," from John Myslicki, chief, transboundary movement division, to Michael Holly, manager at Philip's Parkdale yard in Hamilton. The documents are silent on the waste's ultimate disposal destination, a key failing according to critics.
17 The internecine battle scraped the gutter when the Bosvelds served notice they intended to sue me for libel over an angry union bulletin I'd written after the firing of the second bargaining committee member, a long-serving union activist. When my transfer grievance reached arbitration, the arbitrator, Bill Kaplan, told me the company was prepared to pay me $50,000 to scram if I agreed to change our contract's language on job postings—a proposition I rejected outright. I instead settled for a deal giving me one month off to write a story of my choice (ultimately on the plethora of industrial toxins Hamilton is sending into Lake Ontario via its sewage treatment plant, an exposé that ironically netted me four awards, including the Ontario Community Newspaper Association's Reporter of the Year). During the next round of negotiations, the company tabled a slew of concessions that quickly became known on our side of the table as "Richard clauses." Many, but not all, addressed job postings and reassignments, and the resulting contract did see some of our language weakened. Cal Bosveld was determined that no union—or perhaps, more importantly, no arbitrator—would ever tell him who to assign where.

18 Ontario Ministry of the Environment, "Taro East Quarry Waste Disposal Site Report on Alleged Receipt of Hazardous Waste Generated by Cyanokem Inc. of Detroit, Michigan," September 1999.
19 Andrew Dreschel, "War of Words: In the Battle over Taro's Controversial Dump, It's Difficult to Separate the Truth from the Hype," *Hamilton Spectator,* 4 May 1996. During this period, the Spectator generally reserved its front page and section for national and international news.
20 Andrew Dreschel, "Talking Tough: Philip Environmental Meets Gossip Head On," *Hamilton Spectator,* 6 May 1996.
21 Andrew Dreschel, "Uncharted Waters: Philip Pays a Price for Going Where Others Would Not," *Hamilton Spectator,* 6 May 1996.
22 An 18 March 1996 letter from Antonio Pingue, Philip senior vice-president of corporate and government affairs, to Hardy Wong, director of the ministry's west central region, states that 9,400 tonnes were dumped between January and June 1995.
23 Memorandum from Gilles Castonguay to Dr. Dennis Corr, chief (A), ministry approvals and planning, West Central Region, 5 February 1996.
24 Job interview, 23 June 1999, in Robbins's office at the *Hamilton Spectator.* Roger Gillespie, an assignment editor, sat in on the interview and said little, although his face turned beet-red during discussion of my Taro coverage. Gillespie has since become the managing editor.

Chapter 5
1 Document available from http://www.rsc.ca/foodbiotechnology/indexEN.html
2 All CBAC reports are available from its Web site: http://cbac-cccb.ca/
3 Press release available from http://www.jic.bbsrc.ac.uk/corporate/Media_and_Public/ Releases/020918.htm
4 Article available from http://www.monsanto.co.uk/news/ukshowlib.phtml?uid=6671
5 In a March 29, 2001, lower court decision, Schmeiser was found guilty

of (a) having Monsanto's patented Roundup Ready gene in canola on his land and (b) not advising Monsanto to come and remove it. A September 4, 2002, Appeals Court ruling (http://decisions.fct-cf.gc.ca/fct/2002/2002fca309.html) upheld the original judgment, and Schmeiser is now seeking leave to appeal to the Supreme Court of Canada. This is a major, precedent-setting case that will affect not simply the hundreds of farmers being charged by Monsanto with patent infringement. Although the patented genes are demonstrably uncontainable, the farmer has been found guilty of their simple presence on his land. These findings bear directly on the whole issue of corporate patent rights versus individual property rights

[6] A technology use agreement, which must be signed in order to buy Monsanto's GM seed.

[7] *Manitoba Co-operator,* 58(46), 4.

Chapter 6

[1] For greater detail, see Donald C. Savage, "Academic Freedom and Institutional Autonomy" in *Troubled Times: Academic Freedom in New Zealand,* ed. R. Crozier, pp. 7–225 (New Zealand: Dunmore Press, 2000). See also Brian Easton, *The Commercialisation of New Zealand* (Auckland: Auckland University Press, 1997) and Ruth Butterworth and Nicholas Tarling, *A Shakeup Anyway: Government and the Universities in a Decade of Reform* (Auckland: Auckland University Press, 1994) (hereafter Butterworth and Tarling).

[2] New Zealand Business Round Table, *Submission on a Future Tertiary Education Policy for New Zealand: Tertiary Education Review* December 1997 (hereafter *1997 Submission*).

[3] *A Future Education Policy for New Zealand: Tertiary Education Review,* Ministry of Education, 1998 (Green Paper); *Tertiary Education in New Zealand: Policy Directions for the 21st Century,* Wellington: Ministry of Education, 1998 (White Paper).

[4] Meredith Edwards, "Review of New Zealand Tertiary Education Institution Governance," (Wellington, New Zealand, Ministry of Education, 2003).

[5] *1997 Submission.*

[6] Butterworth and Tarling, chapter 11.

7. In Canada, the Supreme Court has declared that universities are private institutions and therefore, for example, the federal Charter of Rights does not apply. *McKinney v University of Guelph*, 3 *Supreme Court Reports* (1990), 229.
8. The Victoria University authorities took action against Lally, threatening dismissal, but eventually the parties settled with an agreement to keep the details private before the case was heard by the Employment Tribunal.
9. Simon Jenkins, "A bewildered tribe," *Times Higher Education Supplement*, 19 October 2001.
10. See, for example, accounting firms' involvement in the Enron and Parmalat scandals.
11. Oliver Bertin, "Accounting firms prefer rules to laws," *Globe and Mail*, 22 October 2002.
12. Noel Annan, *The Dons: Mentors, Eccentrics and Geniuses* (London: HarperCollins, 1999).

Chapter 7

1. James P. Winter, *Democracy's Oxygen: How Corporations Control the News* (Montreal: Black Rose Books, 1997).
2. Document available from http://www.ekos.ca
3. See http://www.ekos.ca; http://www.ipsosreid.com (Canada); http://www.Environics.ca
4. Personal interview for *Winnipeg Free Press* column published 18 August 1995.
5. See http://www.ekos.ca, *loc.cit.*
6. CBC Online News, "CanWest Fires Ottawa Citizen's Publisher," 17 June 2002, available from http://www.ottawa.cbc.ca/newsinreview/june/jun17.html
7. John Miller, *Yesterday's News: Why Canada's Daily Newspapers Are Failing Us* (Halifax: Fernwood, 1998).

Chapter 9

1. Concordia University Board of Governor Minutes September 18, 2002. Mrs. Vineberg informed the assembly that during *Closed Session*, the Board of Governors adopted a document entitled 'A

Cooling-off period at Concordia University' together with a Policy on the Treatment of Student Disciplinary Matters in Exceptional Cases. The Board also passed a resolution regarding information and display tables in the Hall Building. The details of the aforementioned resolutions and Policy will be disclosed to the University community later this day.
2   Code of Student Conduct, enacted July 1, 2002.
3   Document available from http://www.uottawa.ca/students/community/ policies/ucu.html

Chapter 10
1   Survey prepared by the IFJ, 2002, available from http://www.ifj.org
2   Canadian Journalists for Free Expression, *Not in the Newsroom! CanWest Global and Free Expression* (Toronto: CJFE, 2002).
3   Statistics available from TNG-Canada: www.tngcanada.org
4   Ibid.
5   Robert W. McChesney, *Rich Media, Poor Democracy Rich Media, Poor Democracy: Communication Politics in Dubious Times* (Urbana and Chicago: University of Illinois Press, 1999).
6   Interview with Dan Rather, BBC News, 6 June 2002.
7   George Orwell, *Essays* (Harmondsworth, Mddx. Penguin Modern Classics, 1980).
8   Full details of the proposed new laws are available from http://www.statewatch.org/news/index.html
9   The TNG-CWA union created a special Web log of cases of media victims during this period. It is available from www.newsguild.org

Chapter 11
1   Voltaire, *Eléments de la philosophie de Newton* (Amsterdam: E. Ledet, 1738).
2   S. Chandrasekhar, *Eddington* (Cambridge: Cambridge University Press, 1983).
3   J. Thompson, P. Baird, and J. Downie, *The Olivieri Report: The Complete Text of the Report of the Independent Inquiry Commissioned by the Canadian Association of University Teachers* (Toronto: Lorimer, 2001); D. Healy, *Let Them Eat Prozac* (Toronto: Lorimer, 2003).

4   Thompson, Baird and Downie. *The Olivieri Report*.
5   F. Furet, *Revolutionary France, 1770–1880* (Oxford: Blackwell Publishers, 1995).
6   V. Fowke and B. Laskin, "Report of the investigation … into the dismissal of Professor H. S. Crowe …," *CAUT Bulletin* 7, no. 3 (1959): 3–50, plus appendices.

Bibliography

Introduction

Johnson, C. (2004). "Ex-Enron Accountant Causey Indicted." *The Washington Post*, p. E1.

Stern, C. (2004). "WorldCom Wraps up Restatements." *The Washington Post*, p. E3.

Chapter 1

Anderson, J. L. (1991). Rushton's racial comparisons: An ecological critique of theory and method. *Canadian Psychology, 32,* 51–60.

Berenthal, B. I. (2002). Challenges and opportunities in the psychological sciences. *American Psychologist, 57,* 215–218.

Best, J. (2001). *La subversion silencieuse: Censure, autocensure et lutte pour la liberté d'expression.* Montreal: Les Éditions Balzac.

Coleman, A. L., & Alger, J. R. (1996). Beyond speech codes: Harmonizing rights of free speech and freedom from discrimination on university campuses. *Journal of College and University Law, 23,* 91–132.

Dahlin, K. (1993, February 8). An article of little faith: A controversy of grand proportions. *University of Toronto Bulletin,* pp. 8–9.

Dallum, S. J., Gleaves, D. H., Cepeda-Benito, A., Silberg, J. L., Kraemer, H., & Spiegel, D. (2001). The effects of child sexual abuse: Comment on Rind, Tromovitch, and Bauserman (1998). *Psychological Bulletin, 127,* 715–733.

Dancik, B. P. (1991). Note to readers. *Canadian Journal of Physics, 69,* 1403.

Dancik, B. P. (1993). Learning from error. *Scholarly Publishing, 24,* 269–273.

Fowler, R. D. (1999). *APA letter to the honorable Rep. DeLay (R-Tx).* Cited in Lilienfeld, 2002.

Freeman, G. (1990). Kinetics of nonhomogeneous processes in human society: Unethical behaviour and social chaos. *Canadian Journal of Physics, 68,* 794–798.

Garrison, E. G., & Kobor, P. C. (2002). Weathering a political storm: A contextual perspective on a psychological research controversy. *American Psychologist, 57,* 165–175.

Horn, M. (1999). *Academic freedom in Canada: A history.* Toronto: University of Toronto Press.

Lilienfeld, S. (2002). When worlds collide: Social science, politics, and the Rind et al. (1998) child sexual abuse meta-analysis. *American Psychologist, 57,* 176–188.

McCarty, R. (2002). Science, politics, and peer review: An editor's dilemma. *American Psychologist, 57,* 198–201.

Minois, G. (1995). *Censure et culture sous l'Ancien Régime.* Paris: Fayard.

Montagnes, I. (1993). Introduction to the issue: The Freeman affair. *Scholarly Publishing, 24,* 193–203.

National Research Council of Canada. (1993). A new publications policy for the NRC. *Scholarly Publishing, 24,* 274–280.

Phillips, D. (2002). Collisions, logrolls, and psychological science. *American Psychologist, 57,* 219–221.

Rauch, J. (1999). Washington's other sex scandal. *National Journal, 31,* 2269–2270.

Rind, B., Tromovitch, P., & Bauserman, R. (1998). A meta-analytic examination of assumed properties of child sexual abuse using college samples. *Psychological Bulletin, 124,* 22–53.

Rind, B., Tromovitch, P., & Bauserman, R. (2001). The validity and appropriateness of methods, analyses, and conclusions of Rind et al. (1993): A rebuttal of victimological critique from Ondersma et al. (2001) and Dallam et al. (2001). *Psychological Bulletin, 127,* 734–758.

Rushton, J. P. (1989). *Evolutionary biology and heritable traits.* Paper presented at the Annual Meeting of the American Association for the Advancement of Science, San Francisco, CA.

Rushton, J. P. (1991). Do r-K strategies underlie human race differences? *Canadian Psychology, 32,* 29–42.

Schafer, A. (1989, March 9). Opposite sides of the same coin: Salman Rushdie and Philippe Rushton. *The Globe and Mail,* p. A7.

Sheinin, R. (1993). Academic freedom and integrity and ethics in publishing. *Scholarly Publishing, 24,* 232–247.

Sher, K. J., & Eisenberg, N. (2002). Publication of Rind et al. (1998): The editors' perspective. *American Psychologist, 57,* 206–210.

Sternberg, R. J. (2002). Everything you need to know to understand the current controversies you learned from psychological research: A comment on the Rind and Lilienfeld controversies. *American Psychologist, 57,* 193–197.

Suzuki, D (1989, February 11). Defence of Rushton 'right' is propping up faulty work. *The Globe and Mail,* p. D4.

Weizmann, F., Wiener, N. I., Wiesenthal, D. L., & Ziegler, M. (1990). Differential K theory and racial hierarchies. *Canadian Psychology, 32,* 1–13.

Weizmann, F., Wiener, N. I., Wiesenthal, D. L., & Ziegler, M. (1991). Eggs, eggplants and eggheads: A rejoinder to Rushton. *Canadian Psychology, 32,* 43–50.

Wolfe, M. (1991, September 3). Important issues unresolved in 'Freeman controversy' argues Morris Wolfe. *The Globe and Mail,* p. D1.

Chapter 3

Adam, B., Beck, U., & Van Loon, J. (2000). *The risk society and beyond: Critical issues in social theory.* London: Sage.

Alderman, J., Wolkow, R., Chung, M., & Johnston, H. F. (1998). Sertraline treatment of children and adolescents with OCD or depression: Pharmacokinetics, tolerability, and efficacy. *Journal of the American Academy of Child & Adolescent Psychiatry, 37,* 386–394.

Bass, A. (1999, October 4). Drug companies enrich Brown professor. *Boston Globe,* p. A1.

Berman, E. S. (1999). Too little bone: The medicalization of osteoporosis. *Journal of Woman's Health and Law, 1,* 257–277.

Current Medical Directions. (1999, January 29). Worldwide publications status update: Zoloft (Sertraline HCL). (Document available from author.)

Dumit, J. (2003, July). Pharmaceutical witnessing: Drugs for life and direct-to-consumer advertising in an era of surplus health. Paper presented at the Association of Social Anthropology Decennial Conference: Anthropology and Science, Manchester, England.

Frank, T. (2000). *One market under God.* New York: Anchor.

Glenmullen, J. (2000). *Prozac backlash.* New York: Simon & Schuster.

Healy, D. (1993). *Images of trauma.* London: Faber & Faber.

Healy, D. (1998). *The antidepressant era.* Cambridge: Harvard University Press.

Healy, D. (1999). Antidepressant psychopharmacotherapy: At the crossroads. *International Journal of Psychiatry in Clinical Practice, 3,* S9–S15.

Healy, D. (2000a). Antidepressant induced suicidality. *Primary Care Psychiatry, 6,* 23–28.

Healy, D. (2000b). Good science or good business? Hastings Center Report, 30, 19–22.

Healy, D., Savage, M., Michael, P., Harris, M., Hirst, D., Carter, et al. (2001). Psychiatric bed utilisation: 1896 and 1996 compared. *Psychological Medicine, 31,* 779–790.

Healy, D. (2002). The creation of psychopharmacology. Cambridge: Harvard University Press.

Healy, D. (2003a). Lines of evidence on SSRIs and risk of suicide. *Psychotherapy and Psychosomatics, 72,* 71–79.

Healy, D. (2003b). *Let them eat Prozac.* Toronto: Lorimer,

Healy, D., & Cattell, D. (2003). The interface between authorship, industry and science in the domain of therapeutics. *British Journal of Psychiatry, 182,* 22–27.

Just how tainted has medicine become? (2002). *Lancet, 359,* 1167. (See also responses in How tainted is medicine? *Lancet, 359,* 1775–1776.)

Bibliography

Kasper, S. (1999). Bridging the gap between psychopharmacology and clinical symptoms. *International Journal of Psychiatry in Clinical Practice, 3*(Suppl. 2), 17–20.

Keller, M. B., Ryan, N. D., Strober, M. et al. (2001). Efficacy of paroxetine in the treatment of adolescent major depression: A randomized, controlled trial. *Journal of the American Academy of Child and Adolescent Psychiatry, 40,* 762–772.

La Rossa, J., Jr, & Romano, G. (2000). Boss of bosses: Charles B. Nemeroff, MD, PhD. *Economics of Neuroscience, 2,* 8.

Lemmens, T., & Freedman, B. (2000). Ethics review for sale? Conflict of interest and commercial research review boards. *Milbank Quarterly, 78,* 547–584.

Lenzner, R., & Kellner, T. (2000, November 27). Corporate saboteurs. *Forbes,* 157–168.

Lopez-Ibor, J. J. (1993). Reduced suidality on paroxetine. *European Psychiatry, 1*(Suppl. 8), 17s–19s.

Malt, U. F., Robak, O. H., Madsbu, H-B, Bakke, O., & Loeb, M. (1999). The Norwegian naturalistic treatment study of depression in general practice (NORDEP). I: Randomized double-blind study. *British Medical Journal, 318,* 1180–1184.

Montgomery, S. A., Dunner, D. L., & Dunbar, G. (1995). Reduction of suicidal thoughts with paroxetine in comparison to reference antidepressants and placebo. *European Neuropsychopharmacology, 5,* 513.

Motus v. Pfizer, Inc. 196F. Supp. 2d 984 (C.D. Cal. 2001); and the same parties, US Court of Appeals, 9th Circuit, arg. Oct 10, 2004, filed Feb. 9, 2004, and briefs, viz. 02-55372 and 02-55498.

Pfizer Expert Report. (1997, October 20). Sertraline hydrochloride for obsessive compulsive disorder in paediatric patients. (Document available from author.)

Rampton, S., & Stauber, J. (2001). *Trust us, we're experts!* New York: Tarcher-Putnam.

Stauber, J., & Rampton, S. (1995). Toxic sludge is good for you: Lies, damn lies and the public relations industry. Monroe, ME: Common Courage Press.

Teen depression: 3 million kids suffer from it. What you can do.

(2002, October 7). *Newsweek*, 52–61.

Thase, M. E., Entsuah, A. R., & Rudolph, R. L. (2001). Remission rates during treatment with venlafaxine or SSRIs. *British Journal of Psychiatry, 178*, 234–241. (See also Correspondence: Conflict of interest and the *British Journal of Psychiatry*. *British Journal of Psychiatry, 180*, 82–83.)

Tollefson, G. D., & Rosenbaum, J. F. (1998). Selective serotonin reuptake inhibitors. In A. F. Schatzberg & C. B. Nemeroff (Eds.), The American psychiatric press textbook of psychopharmacology (pp. 219–237). Washington, DC: APA Press.

Tranter, R., Healy, H., Cattell, D., & Healy, D. (2002). Functional variations in agents differentially selective to monoaminergic systems. *Psychological Medicine, 32*, 517–524.

Tranter, R., O'Donovan, C., Chandarana, P., & Kennedy, S. (2002). Prevalence and outcome of partial remission in depression. *Journal of Psychiatry and Clinical Neuroscience, 27*, 241–247.

Chapter 5

Abley, M. (2000, March 28). Magazine insert leaves a bad taste: Ottawa pushes safety of bio-engineered food. *Montreal Gazette* p. A1.

Buchanan, B., & Chapela, I. Novartis revisited. *California Monthly, 112*(4). Article available from http://www.cnr.berkeley.edu/~christos/espm118/ articles/novartis_revisited_chapela.html

Clark, E. Ann, & Lehman, H. (2001). Assessment of GM crops in commercial agriculture. *Journal of Agricultural and Environmental Ethics, 14*, 3–28.

Deegan, D. (2001). *Managing activism: A guide to dealing with activists and pressure groups*. London: The Institute of Public Relations/Kogan Page.

Donovan, J. C., R. E. Morgan, & Potholm, C. P. (1981). *People, power, and politics: An introduction to political science*. Reading, MA: Addison-Wesley.

Freeze, C. (2002, February 5). Ottawa promoting safety of GMOs. *Globe and Mail*, p. A9.

Furtan, H., & Holzman, J. (2001). Agronomic benefits and costs of GMO crops: What do we know? In Richard Gray et al., *Taking stock:*

The benefits and costs of genetically modified crops. Report commissioned by CBAC, available from http://strategis.ic.gc.ca/epic/internet/incbac-cccb.nsf/vwGeneratedInterE/ah00388e.html#part_4

Hager, N., & Burton, B. (1999). *Secrets and lies: The anatomy of an anti-environmental PR campaign.* Monroe, ME: Common Courage Press.

Leiss, W. (2002). *In the chamber of risks: Understanding risk controversies.* Montreal: McGill-Queen's University Press.

Little, A. (1990, June). A green corporate image—more than a logo. Paper presented at the Green Marketing Conference, Sydney, Australia.

Morriss, J. (2001, June 21) Rude Science. *Manitoba Co-operator, 58*(46), 4.

Orr, D. W. (1994). *Earth in mind: On education, environment, and the human prospect.* Washington, DC: Island Press.

Orwell, G. (1949). *1984.* Oxford: Clarendon Press.

Rampton, S., & Stauber, J. (2001). *Trust us, we're experts!* New York: Tarcher-Putnam.

Toomey, G. (2002, October). Letting the gene out of the bottle. *University Affairs,* 20–25.

Wiesel, E. (1990). Remarks before the Global Forum, Moscow. Cited in D. Orr, *Earth in mind: On education, environment, and the human prospect* (p. 213). Washington, DC: Island Press.

Chapter 8

Bagdikian, Ben H. (1997). *The media monopoly,* 5th ed. Boston: Beacon Press.

Carroll, William K., & Shaw, Murray. (2001). Consolidating a neo-liberal policy bloc in Canada, 1976 to 1996. *Canadian Public Policy, 27*(2), 196–216.

Clement, Wallace (1975). *The Canadian corporate elite: An analysis of economic power.* Toronto: McClelland & Stewart.

Curran, James. (1979). Capitalism and control of the press, 1800–1975. In J. Curran, M. Gurevitch, & J. Woollacott (Eds.), *Mass communication and society* (pp. 195–230). Beverly Hills: Sage.

Curran, James. (1996). Mass media and democracy revisited. In James Curran & Michael Gurevitch (Eds.), *Mass media and society,* 2nd ed.

(pp. 81–119). London: Arnold.

Gandy, Oscar H. (1982). *Beyond agenda setting: Information subsidies and public policy.* Norwood, NJ: Ablex.

Gans, Herbert J. (1980). *Deciding what's news.* New York: Vintage.

Gutstein, Donald, with Robert Hackett & NewsWatch Canada. (1998). *Question the* Sun! *A content analysis of diversity in the* Vancouver Sun *before and after the Hollinger take-over.* Burnaby, BC: School of Communication, Simon Fraser University.

Hackett, Robert A. (1991). *News and dissent: The press and the politics of peace in Canada.* Norwood, NJ: Ablex.

Hackett, Robert A. (2000). Taking back the media: Notes on the potential for a communicative democracy movement. *Studies in Political Economy, 63,* 61–86.

Hackett, Robert A. (2001a). News media and civic equality: Watch dogs, mad dogs, or lap dogs? In Edward Broadbent (Ed.), *Democratic equality: What went wrong?* (pp. 198–212). Toronto: University of Toronto Press.

Hackett, Robert. (2001b). Covering up the "War on Terrorism": The master frame and the media chill. *Media, (8)*3, 8–11.

Hackett, Robert A., & Gruneau, Richard, with Gutstein, Donald, Gibson, Timothy A., & Newswatch Canada. (2000). *The missing news: Filters and blind spots in Canada's press.* Ottawa: Canadian Centre for Policy Alternatives/Toronto: Garamond Press.

Hackett, Robert A., & Uzelman, Scott. (2002). Tracing corporate influences on the press: A summary of recent NewsWatch Canada research. *Journalism Studies, 4*(3), 331–346.

Hackett, Robert A., & Zhao, Yuezhi. (1998). *Sustaining democracy?: Journalism and the politics of objectivity.* Toronto: Garamond Press.

Hallin, Daniel C. (1996). Commercialism and professionalism in the American news media. In James Curran & Michael Gurevitch (Eds.), *Mass media and society,* 2nd ed. (pp. 243–262). London: Arnold.

Herman, Edward S., & McChesney, Robert W. (1997). *The global media: The new missionaries of global capitalism.* New York: Pantheon Books.

McChesney, Robert W. (1999). *Rich media, poor democracy: Communication politics in dubious times.* Urbana and Chicago: University of Illinois Press.

Bibliography

Miller, John. (2001). Review of the missing news. *Canadian Journal of Communication, 25*(4), 574–576.

Mosdell, Jackie. (1997). *Globe and Mail* has the "right stuff." *NewsWatch Monitor, 1*(3), iii. Article available from http://newswatch.cprost.sfu.ca/monitor/issue1.html#mosdell

Roberts, Anne. (1993, October). All the news we can manage. *New Directions,* 30.

Shoemaker, Pamela J., & Reese, Stephen D. (1996). *Mediating the message: Theories of influences on mass media content,* 2nd ed. New York: Longman.

Smythe, Dallas. (1981). *Dependency road: Communications, capitalism, consciousness and Canada.* Norwood, NJ: Ablex.

Soley, Lawrence. (2002). *Advertising censorship.* Milwaukee: Southshore Press.

Underwood, Doug. (1995). *When MBAs rule the newsroom: How the marketers and managers are reshaping today's media.* New York: Columbia University Press.

Winter, James P. (1997). *Democracy's oxygen: How corporations control the news.* Montreal: Black Rose Books.

Index

academic freedom, 11–13, 170, 179–80, 189–90; privatization and, 129–31. *See also* freedom of expression
academics: and corporate pressure, 161, 185–90; and journalists, 15; lack of political engagement, 43–50; and protection of civil liberties, 19; task of intellectuals, 45
access to information, 8; commodification of knowledge, 160; restrictions, 8; for surveillance, 9–10
accounting firms, influence of, 129, 133
adult-child sex, 29–32
advertising, 77–78, 149–51, 158
advocacy reporting, 104

affluent audiences, 150, 151
Agriculture and Agri-Food Canada (AAFC), 112
air travel, security measures, 9
Alger, J.R., 34, 36
American Association for the Advancement of Science (AAAS), 24, 30, 31
American Civil Liberties Union (ACLU), 7, 178
American myth of goodness, 39–40
American Psychiatric Association, 65
American Psychological Association, 29, 30, 31, 36
American Psychologist, 31, 36
American Tobacco Co., 108
American universities: as centres

of knowledge, 46–47; and critical inquiry, 47–50
Ancaster News, 98
Anti-Empire Crowd, 41
anti-feminism, 26–28
Anti-Terrorism Act (Canada), 9
APEC Conference protests, 166
Arar, Maher, 8
arbitrary detention, 8–9

Bain, Anne, 76, 81, 84
Baird, Patricia, 186
Beecroft, Stephen, 77, 85, 86, 87, 89, 96
Berenthal, Bennett, 34
Berlusconi, Silvio, 172
Bernays, Edward, 107–8
biometric identifiers, 10
Biotechnology in Canada, 112–13
Black, Conrad, 89, 97, 139, 140
Boston Globe, 62
Bosveld, Cal, 89, 92, 96–97
Bosveld, Ken, 97–98
Brabant Newspapers, 76
British Association for Psychopharmacology, 56
British College of Psychiatrists, 65–66
British Columbia: disciplining dissent, 170
British Journal of Psychiatry, 60
British Medical Journal, 63
Broom, David, 83
Bunyan, Tony, 176
Burson Marsteller, 111
Bush, George W., 39–40

C. D. Howe Institute, 152
Calami, Peter, 140
Calgary Herald, 97
campus protests, 165–70
Canadian Association of Physicists, 28
Canadian Association of University Teachers, 9, 25, 168, 188–89
Canadian Bar Association, 10
Canadian Biotechnology Advisory Committee (CBAC), 113–14
Canadian Centre for Policy Alternatives, 154
Canadian Federation of Students, 167, 168
Canadian Food Inspection Agency (CFIA), 112
Canadian Journal of Physics, 26, 27
Canadian Living, 112
Canadian Psychological Association, 27
CanWest, 172, 173
CanWest Global, 141
Cashore, Harvey, 84
Cattrell, Dinah, 62
CBC, 80, 81, 84, 154
censorship, 36–37, 139–41
Center for Media and Democracy, 53
Center for Media and Public Affairs, 157
Chamberlain Communications Group, 56, 57
Chapela, Ignacio, 117

215

Charles X, 187
Choice Point, 10
Chomsky, Noam, 135
Chrétien, Jean, 139, 167
Cité Libre, 187
civil liberties: restrictions, 7–11; upholding, 17–19; war on terrorism and, 176–78
Clark, Brad, 80, 92, 93, 94, 95, 98
class inequality, 157–58
Clement, Wallace, 147–48
clinical trials, 69–73
codes of student conduct, 168–70
Coleman, A.L., 36, 37
commodification of knowledge, 160
Common Sense Revolution, 96
Communications, Energy and Paperworkers Union of Canada (CEP), 188, 189
Competitive Enterprise Institute, 116
Concordia University, 167–68
Conko, Greg, 116
consumerism, 151
Consumers' Association of Canada, 112
"consumer sovereignty," 149–50
contract research organizations (CROs), 72
contracts. *See* informed consent *vs.* contracts, in clinical trials
Copps, Geraldine, 103
Corlett, John, 167

corporate control: and academic freedom, 12–13; constraints on journalists, 139–42; and education, 127–32; and freedom of expression, 12; and government agenda, 16; and public interests, 135–37. *See also* media
corporate crime. *See* white-collar crime
Coup de Pouce, 112
Cousin, Victor, 187
Cripps, Mark, 96
CTV, 94, 154
Cultural Doves, 41, 42–43
Current Medical Directions (CMD), 61–65
cyanide waste shipments, 92–95, 100
Cyanokem Inc., 92–93, 93

Daily Telegraph, 150
Dancik, Bruce P., 27, 28
Database Technologies, 10
Davey Commission, 139
Davies, Libby, 168
DeLay, Tom, 30
depoliticization, of editorial content, 150–51
diseases, "selling," 66–69
dissent: campus protests, 165–70; defined, 143; intolerance for, 7–8, 168–90, 177; and media, 160
Dixie Chicks, 8
doublespeak: 105–23; academic

applications of, 115–23; government applications of, 111–16; industrial applications of, 107–11; and Orwell, 106–7; and public relations firms, 107–10; third-party technique, 110–11, 121
doublethink, 106
Downie, Jocelyn, 186
Doyle, Ed, 95–96
Dreschel, Andrew, 101–2
Dumit, Joseph, 69
Dundas Star, 98
Dunsford, John, 77, 86
Duplessis, Maurice, 187
Duplisea, Brad, 112

Eddington, Arthur, 186
Edelman Public Relations Worldwide, 108
Edmonton Journal, 137
education, business model of, 127–32
Education Act (New Zealand), 130
Ekos Research, 135, 136, 137
elective affinity, 147–48, 154–55
electric arc furnace dust, 92, 102–3
Eli Lilly, 56–58, 66
Elliott, Brenda, 81
Ellis, Brian, 115
Emory University, 31
Engler, Yves, 168
Environmental Assessment Board, 74

Environmental Protection Agency, 92
Ernst and Young, 129, 133
European Union: and war on terrorism, 176

FBI, 177, 178
Ferrara, Chad, 80
Fifth Estate, 80, 81, 84
Fisher, Gordon, 86
Fisher, John, 77, 85, 99
Food and Drug Administrtion (FDA), 66
Food Biotechnology Communications Network (FBCN), 112
Fowler, Raymond, 30
Fracassi, Allen, 80, 82, 101–2
Fracassi, Philip, 101
Fraser Institute, 152, 154, 157
freedom of expression: corporate intimidation and, 77–78, 83–88, 95; free speech, 170; and journalism, 12, 171–72; media concentration and, 12, 139–42, 172–73; more-speech approach, 34–37; war on terrorism and, 173–75
Freeman, Gordon, 26–28, 33
free speech. *See* academic freedom
free trade, 137–39
Furtan, Harley, 114

Gateway, 28

217

genetic modification (GM), 112–23
ghost-written scientific papers: as infomercials, 61–65; manipulation of data, 63–64; in pharmaceutical industry, 55, 59–61; prevalence of, 63
GlaxoSmithKline, 58, 65
Glenmullen, Joseph, 56–57
globalization: universalizations claims, 70
Globe and Mail, 154, 155
Le Globe, 187
governments, and corporate power, 136–37
Grants Pass Daily Courier, 177
Graves, Frank, 137
Guizot, François, 187
Guthrie, Dan, 177
Gutting, Tom, 177

Hamilton Region Conservation Authority, 79, 88
Hamilton Spectator, 75–76, 83, 94, 101–4
harassment, defined, 36
Harris, Mike, 75, 96, 98, 100
Hastings Center, 58
Hastings Center Report, 57
Hawks, 41, 42
Healy, David, 53–73
Herron, Don, 146
Herron, Shaun, 103
Hilson, Michael, 81–83, 92–93, 95
Hodgson, Bob, 76

Honderich, John, 89
Hughes, Leslie, 141

informed consent *vs.* contracts, in clinical trials, 71
Institutional Review board (IRD) system, 72
intellectuals. *See* academics; journalists
International Civil Liberties Monitoring Group, 9
International Federation of Journalists (IFJ), 171, 175, 176, 187
International Freedom of Expression Exchange (IFEX), 180
investigative journalism, 156–57
Iraq, invasion of, 19–20
It's Your Call, 84

JAMA (Journal of the American Medical Association), 63
John Innes Centre, 116
journalists: and academics, 15, 185–90; influence on media, 145, 147–48; and protection of civil liberties, 19; right wing bias of, 134–35, 147–149. *See also* freedom of expression; media
Journal of Psychiatry and Clinical Neuroscience, 61
Journal of the American Academy of Child and Adolescent Psychiatry, 63

Keller, Martin, 58, 59, 62
Kent Commission, 139, 185
Kuhn, Thomas, 64

Labour Party of New Zealand, 128, 129, 131
Lally, Martin, 131
Lancet, The, 60
LaPointe, Kirk, 94, 104
Leiss, Bill, 114
Leitner, Richard, 74–104
Leroux, Pierre, 187
Leslie, David, 129, 133
Lévesque, René, 187–88
libel chill, 83–84
Library of Congress, 11
Lilienfeld, Scott, 31–32, 36
Lilly. *See* Eli Lilly
Los Angeles Times, 108
Losani, Fred, 91–92

Mackie, Marlene, 27
Maclean's, 90, 93
Malt, U.F., 63
market liberal hegemony, 151–52
McAulay, Lawrence, 142
McCarthy, Richard, 31–32
McChesney, Robert, 175
McGuinty, Dalton, 96
McKay, Dennis, 99
media: business coverage, 153–54; conservative bias of journalists, 147–48; corporate pressures, 159; corporatization of, 137–39; coverage of war on terrorism, 12, 173–75; extra-media influences, 146, 149–51; ideological influence, 146, 151–52; influences on, 145–52; labour, 153–54; "left-liberal bias" myth, 156–57; media concentration, 139–41, 172–73; need for diversity, 169; neglected issues, 157–59; newsroom work routines, 145–46, 148–49; 9/11 blind spots, 144–45; organizational imperatives, 146, 148–49; self-censorship, 158, 175. *See also* freedom of expression
Mediaset, 172
medical-writing agencies, 61–62, 72. *See also* ghost-written scientific papers
Medicines Control Agency (MCA), 66
Memorial University, 167
Mesmer, Franz, 54
Michener Award, 88–90
Microsoft, 108
Military recruiting, 168
Miller, John, 140
Mills, Russell, 139–41
Minois, Georges, 36
Monsanto, 107, 117–22
Montreal Gazette, 137, 173
more-speech approach, 34–37
Morriss, John, 122
Morrow, Mark, 83
Murdoch, Peter, 189
Murphy, Laura W., 178

National Academy of Sciences, 30
National Coalition for Universities in the Public Interest, 170
National Identity Card, 10
National Institute of Nutrition, 112
National Media Archive, 157
National Party of New Zealand, 128, 129, 132
National Research Council Journals, 27–28
Nemeroff, Charles, 56, 58
Netanyahu, Benjamin, 168
New Democratic Party, 168
newspeak, 106
newsroom work routines, 145–46, 148–49
NewsWatch Canada, 152, 154, 155, 158, 159
Newton, Issac, 186
New York Times, 108
New Zealand: electoral system, 128, 132; neo-conservative reforms, 127–32
New Zealand Business Round Table, 128–29
Nicol, John, 93
9/11 coverage, 144–45
Nixon, Richard, 111
Nobel, David, 170
Nojeim, Gregory T., 178
Novartis (Syngenta), 116
null hypothesis, 69

objectivity, ethos of, 149
Olivieri, Nancy, 13
Olivieri Committee of Inquiry, 186–87
Ontario Human Rights Commission, 25–26
Ontario Ministry of Education and Training, 36
Ontario Municipal Board, 80
Organisation of American States, 2001 meetings, 166–67
Orr, David, 123
Orwell, George, 175
Ott, Terry, 83, 84
Ottawa Citizen, 139

Palango, Paul, 84, 87–88, 92–93
Patriot Act (US), 8, 177–78
Paul, Ross, 167
Pearl, Daniel, 175
Peterson, David, 25
Petro Chem, 93
Pfizer, 59, 65, 66
pharmaceutical industry: and clinical trials, 69–72; manipulation of data, 63–64; marketing tactics, 53–73; medical risk management, 66–69; and mood disorders, 65–66, 70; promotional perks, 64; regulatory bodies, 71–72; suppression of data, 70
PhilipServices Corp., 74–104
Phillips, Deborah, 34
Pinel, Philippe, 54
Pingue, Antonio, 77

Pioneer Fund, 32
political correctness, 27
Political Doves-with-Wings-Pinned, 41, 43–46
political funding, 139
Porter/Novelli, 110
poverty, 157–58
Prakash, C.S., 116
Prescott Journal, 96
prescriptions, purpose of, 72
PricewaterhouseCoopers, 129
privacy, incursions on, 9–10
privatization: and academic freedom, 129–31; corporate agenda, 136
Prozac, 56–57, 58–59
Prudhomme, Stephen, 28
psychiatry, 53–55
Psychological Bulletin, 29, 30, 31
public relations companies, 107–111
Public Relations Society of America (PRSA), 111

qualitative research, 27
"quality" pharmaceutical product, 68
Queen Street Mental Health Facility, 54

race, and genetics, 23–26
Rampton, Sheldon, 53–54, 110, 111
Rather, Dan, 175
Rauch, J., 37
RCMP, 166–67

Reagan, Ronald, 152
research, and corporate agenda, 131
Resolution 107, 29–30, 31
Rind et al. case, 29–32, 33–34
risks: and access to data, 68; in clinical trials, 70, 73; medical risk management, 66–69
Robbins, Dana, 103–4
Robbins, Tim, 8
Robertson, Gord, 100
Robinson, Svend, 168
Rocoski, George, 93–94
Rose, Merrill, 110
Rosenbaum, 58
Roundup Ready Canola, 118–119
Royal Society of Canada's Panel on the Future of Food Biotechnology, 113, 122
Runciman, Bob, 96
Rushton, J. Philippe, 23–26, 32

Sainsbury Laboratory, 116
Salmon, Matt, 30
Sarandon, Susan, 8
Schafer, Arthur, 37
Schatzberg, Alan, 58
Schlessinger, Laura, 29
Schmeiser, Peter, 107, 117–22
Schwadron, Robert, 57
Science, 27
security: and civil liberties, 7–11. *See also* war on terrorism
selective serotonin reuptake inhibitor (SSRI) drugs, 56–58, 60, 62–64, 66

September 11 terrorist attacks. *See* 9/11 coverage
sertraline. *See* Zoloft (sertraline)
Shandwick New Zealand, 109
Shoemaker and Reese model, 145–47
sildenafil. *See* Viagara (sildenafil)
Skarica, Toni, 93
Slater, Carl, 93
Society of Harmony, 54
Southam newspaper chain, 76, 140
Space Imaging, 177
spin doctoring. *See* doublespeak
St. Catharines Standard, 97
Stark, Cannie, 27, 33
Statewatch, 176
Stauber, John, 53–54, 110, 111
Sterling, Harry, 156
Sternberg, Robert J., 35
Stoney Creek, 74; city council, 78–79, 95
Stoney Creek Chamber of Commerce, 99
Stoney Creek News, 76–101
Stoney Creek Residents Against Pollution (SCRAP), 77, 80, 87, 92
Suharto, President, 166
Sun newspaper group, 141
surveillance, collection of personal information, 9–10
Suzuki, David, 25
Syngenta, 116

Talan, Jamie, 57

Taro East Quarry Landfill, 75–104
Taro leachate, 103
Taro West Quarry Landfill, 75
Tassé, Roch, 9, 10
Texas City Sun, 177
Thase, Michael, 60, 63
Thatcher, Margaret, 131, 152
"think tanks," neo-liberal, 154, 155
Thompson, Jon, 186–87
Timberlands West Coast Ltd., 109
tobacco industry, 54
Tollefson, 58
Toronto Star, 89, 137, 153
Torstar Corp., 76
"total newspapering," 161
Tranter, Richard, 60
Travers, Jim, 140
Trudeau, Pierre, 187–88
Turkstra, Herman, 78, 81, 83–84, 86
Tuskegee University, 116

Ultra-Hawks, 41–42
University Affairs, 115
University of Alberta, 26, 28
University of California, Berkeley, 116
University of Ottawa, 169–70
University of Texas, 46
University of Toronto, 54, 169
University of Western Ontario, 23, 25
University of Windsor, 166–67

Vancouver Sun, 147, 153, 158
Varangu, Anne, 99
venlafaxine, 60–61
Veri, Victor, 80–81
Viagara (sildenafil), 67
Voltaire, 186

war on terrorism: coverage of, 173–75. *See also* security
Warshaw, 59
Watson, William, 140
Waxman, Robert, 90
Weber, Max, 147
Weizmann, Frederic, 25
White, aidan, 187
white-collar crime, 157
Wiesel, Elie, 123
Wildeman, Alan, 115–16
Willis, Clive, 28
Winkler, Paul, 86, 87
Winnipeg Free Press, 135
Winnipeg Sun, 141
Winter, James, 12
Women in Physics Committee, 28
Wyeth, 60, 61

Young, John, 77, 85–86

Zoloft (sertraline), 62–64